MW01071515

When White Supremacy Knocks, Fight Back!
How White People Can Use their Privilege and How Black People Can Use their Power.

Dr. Wes Bellamy

When White Supremacy Knocks, Fight Back!

Copyright © 2020 by Stokely's Scribes Publishing
All rights reserved. No part of this book may be reproduced,
scanned, or distributed in any printed or electronic form
without permission. First Edition: August 2020 Printed in
the United States of America
ISBN: 978-1-7350287-0-5

Much Love!

Keep Pushing!

DEDICATION

To my baby girl, Stokely Grace Bellamy. You are destined to be more
than a freedom fighter. You are destined to be more than a revolutionary.
You are destined to be yourself. That will always be good enough for
me. Daddy will always fight to make you proud.

When White Supremacy Knocks, Fight Back!

CONTENTS

When White Supremacy Knocks, Fight Back!

ACKNOWLEDGMENTS

Thank you to my Lord and Savior Jesus Christ. Thank you for your mercy, your grace, and your everlasting love. To my wife Ashlee, thank you for being the superwoman behind the scenes that allows me to do the things that I want to do. To my family, thank you for your sacrifice. To my supporters, thank you for the love and encouragement. To my editors and partners, Jennifer Moultrie, Kristin Szakos and KaTera E. Ashford, thank you for giving your time and energy to this project.

To all of my mentors, thank you. To all of the people who have poured positive energy into me, thank you. To all of the people who have spread negativity about me, thank you. To all of the people who have tried to stop what God had planned for me, thank you. My grandmother Evie Mae always told me that I was brave, and I vow to live up to her words.

To the ancestors, please continue to send me the energy to carry out your work. This book. This work. The work ahead, it's all for you.

When White Supremacy Knocks, Fight Back!

1. MY AWAKENING

My Awakening

I'll never forget the first time a White person called me a "nigger." And I'll never forget the look on that police officer's face when he said it.

It was January 18, 2005. I was 19, driving from my mother's home in Atlanta, Georgia, to South Carolina State University in Orangeburg, where I attended college.

I had made the three-hour trek countless times. Usually, I spent the drive in self-reflection, gratitude and thinking about how I had to make my people proud. I had never had any issues.

Until that day.

My 1992 Nissan Sentra wasn't much, but it was mine. I prided myself on keeping the two-door hooptie clean, the windows tinted, and the interior fragrant with my favorite air freshener. It already had 150,000 miles on it when I got it. It couldn't go faster than 70 miles per hour, but I was cool with that.

No matter how my Nissan looked on the outside, I relished in the fact that I was one of the few freshmen on campus who actually had a car.

I hit Interstate 20 in Greene County, Ga., and all that pride, like my self-confidence, shattered in a matter of moments.

I remember spotting the police officer hiding in the cut, setting up what appeared to be a speed trap. I saw him pulling out as two other cars passed me on the highway, accelerating at speeds my Nissan certainly could never aspire to.

I chuckled, relieved that my car couldn't go but so fast, which meant I wouldn't be getting any speeding tickets; or so I thought.

As the officer pulled out onto the road, he began riding beside me. From the corner of my eye, I noticed him looking into my car.

As a young man with all the confidence in the world, who believed wholeheartedly that if you didn't do anything wrong, you'd have nothing to worry about, I nodded at the officer and continued to drive. I was listening to Jeezy's latest mixtape.

The officer pulled ahead of me, but then slowed down and got behind me. I wasn't sure what was happening, but I began to worry.

I knew I wasn't speeding; I couldn't! I was heading back to school and had my student ID with me, along with books positioned in the backseat (*doing that had gotten me out of a few close encounters with the cops a time or two in the past*). I figured if he pulled me over, it would be a quick interaction and I'd be on my way.

Looking back at it, I had already been pulled over so many times, and had had so many encounters with law enforcement, that I was fine with being pulled over again. I was conditioned to believe the police stopping or questioning me was normal.

I was broken before I knew what being broken meant.

As the officer pulled me over and stepped out of his patrol vehicle, a different energy came over me. I'm not sure what it was, but I felt that something wasn't right about this situation.

I hadn't committed any traffic violations. I had traveled in the right lane ("the slow lane," as we called it). Why would he stop me?

The officer approached my vehicle, his hands clasping a gun he trained on me. He ordered me to turn the car off and put my hands outside the window.

I began to sweat, thinking about how I was in the middle of Greene County, Ga., where I didn't know a single person. All I knew was a police officer with a distinct southern drawl held a gun on me.

"Cut off the goddamn car and put your Black ass hands out the window right now," he shouted. "Do it slow, or I swear I'll blow you to pieces right here, right now."

His words sent me into an immediate state of shock, panic and rage. Initially, I compared myself to the many Black brothers and sisters before me who had been kidnapped, beaten, stolen — some of them whisked to places unknown, never to be heard from again.

Then, I tried to steady myself. I told myself this was just a misunderstanding and to stay calm. It would be over soon.

There's a running joke about me in my family. My grandmother, Evie Mae Bellamy, often said, "Wesley is the worst little boy that I have ever met in my whole life. He's the only one that makes me cuss."

I had a temper growing up that I had learned to quell. So, in that moment of sheer terror as the police officer issued commands, gun in hand, I tried to bridle my anger.

The officer got closer to my car. I asked him if I did something wrong, or if I was speeding.

He snarled and barked at me to move very slowly and proctor my driver's license. I already had it out. I handed it to him, along with my college ID. I wanted him to know I was a "good kid."

He took my license, looked at my student ID and threw it back at me through the window.

My fury intensified. I fought the urge to yell, cuss, or fight this man due to his blatant disrespect toward me. Instead, I asked, "Why did you do that?"

His reply was swift and vitriolic: "I don't give a shit where you go to school or *say* you go to school. Get your Black ass out of the car right now."

I struggled to process what was happening. I was enraged, but I also wanted to live. I reluctantly stepped out of the car. The officer asked why the tint on my windows was so dark. He questioned what I had to hide.

I told him I got the windows tinted in South Carolina, where I'm a college student, and my tint met that state's legal standards.

He radioed for backup, telling whomever was listening, "We got us a smart nigger who needs a lesson. Bring the dogs."

Eventually, he holstered his gun, placed me in handcuffs and told me to sit on the hood of my car. He asked for permission to search my vehicle. I refused, telling him that if he didn't have a warrant or probable cause, he didn't have my consent.

He pulled out his gun again and proclaimed that he had arrested "tons of niggers" from South Carolina State University and Benedict College who were running drugs from Atlanta and claimed they were really just returning to school. He was sure I was one of them.

By this time, his partner arrived on scene with a drug dog.

I looked at the younger man and said, "Damn, don't just sit there and let him do this. Yesterday was Martin Luther King Jr.'s birthday."

In hindsight, I have no idea why I said that. Why did I look for sympathy from his partner, from this White man?

From the moment the second officer arrived on scene, I could tell he didn't want any part of what was happening. His face told me he probably wasn't much older than I was. His eyes told me he didn't agree with the situation at all. His silence told me that if I was just quiet, the ordeal would soon be over.

Still, he said nothing to help. He simply let the dog circle my Nissan. Minutes later, he called the canine to him and told his aggressive partner that my car was clean and drug-free.

"I told you that I was in college and I'm going back to school," I told the officer. "You see my books in the backseat. You've seen my ID. I'm not selling drugs. I'm just trying to go back to school. Why are you doing this to me? Yesterday was MLK's birthday for God's sake."

Unmoved and unbothered, he uttered a sentence that still shakes me to my core: "If your Black ass says one more goddamn word, I am going to beat the shit out of you, throw you in my car, and while driving decide if I'm going to take you to my friends or let your raggedy Black ass rot in a cell."

What does one say after that? There's fight or flight. My instincts urged me to fight.

I contemplated what would happen if a physical altercation ensued. Once the cuffs came off, I'd give the officer the best punch to the throat I could throw. But then, once he fell, his partner would rush me, shoot me and the dog would begin to maul me.

I'd either be shot or beaten on the side of the road or taken to jail.

My family, my church members, my neighborhood and all the other people who had poured positivity into my life would be let down.

Every scenario I played out in my mind ended the same way: me losing.

I decided fighting wouldn't work in this situation. That only angered me more - so much so, tears began to fall down my face.

The officer smiled. He took the handcuffs off, told me to sit in my car and wrote me a ticket for my window tint. He threw it in my face, walked back to his car and drove away.

I sat in my Nissan. Paralyzed.

I cried. I screamed. I sank in my seat, engulfed in tears, rage, and pain.

The officer had achieved his goal. He broke me. And in that moment, on the side of the road in rural Georgia, I realized: this is how my ancestors felt. Broken. Ridiculed. Powerless.

That's when I woke up. It was after this awful ordeal on a Georgia highway that I decided I'd figure out a way to help my people never feel what I did. I decided that no one would ever take my power away from me again.

While I'll never forget the words the first officer flung at me, I'll also never forget the look on his partner's face.

He wanted to help but didn't know how. He *should* have spoken up for me. He *should* have had the courage to confront the combative officer. He *should* have used his privilege to come to the defense of another. Why didn't he? Where was his courage?

I've spent several years thinking about this incident. I've also spent the last few years of my life boldly fighting White Supremacy, both covertly and overtly.

And I've had a revelation that I want to share.

A lot of people want to do something about White Supremacy, but don't. A lot of people want to do something about White Supremacy, but don't know how. A lot of people are at the point where they're ready to stand up against White Supremacy, but they're unsure of where to start.

That's why I wrote this book. In it I'll explore ways in which White people, like the backup officer, can take a stand in moments of discomfort and be an ally. For Black people and other people of color, it can be a guide on how to stand up, stay safe, survive these encounters, use our own power to ensure we're not powerless but capable of fighting - and ultimately, defeat White Supremacy once and for all.

Defining White Supremacy

Defining White Supremacy is easy for some but more challenging for others.

It's such a polarizing term that some people fear saying it, so they use words that feel more palatable, like White nationalist.

Even Merriam-Webster struggles with it. The Webster dictionary published the following about White Supremacy:

"We define *White supremacist* as a person who believes that the White race is inherently superior to other races and that White people should have control over people of other races."

In turn, a White nationalist is defined as "one of a group of militant Whites who espouse White Supremacy and advocate enforced racial segregation."

The term is fluid and means different things to different people. But one thing is clear: White Supremacy is perceived very differently in the eyes of Black people and people of color than in the eyes of the majority of White people.

Our challenge today is summoning the courage to move toward a shared lens of how we view White Supremacy and developing the tools to dismantle it.

When White Supremacy knocks on our proverbial doors, do we have the courage to fight back or will we cower?

The first step toward White Supremacy's defeat is wholesale acceptance of the fact that American society has always been rooted in White Supremacy.

We must share the realization that the overwhelming majority of systems — housing, banking, education, law enforcement, etc. — were created from a White supremacist worldview. America has always inherently believed that White people were superior to all others.

That truth is evident in history — from the removal and genocide of the Native Americans on this land, to the first group of enslaved Africans who were stolen by English pirates, brought to Virginia and forced to work alongside indentured servants without the guarantee of freedom. Instead, enslaved people were willed to family members, sold like livestock, and constitutionally marginalized as three-fifths of a person.

Still today, the disparities created by White supremacist-born institutions ripple through communities of color.

After slavery was outlawed, the penal system found a way to recreate it by engineering the mass incarceration crisis that disproportionally imprisons Black and brown men. Years after lynching of Black people fell out of style, Jim Crow-era segregation ensured that Blacks would not and could not receive equal or adequate access to the same sources of wealth, education and housing as their White counterparts.

Those origins of oppression have not dissipated, as evidenced by the murder of nine people at Mother Emanuel Church in Charleston, South Carolina, in 2015 by a man hoping to incite a race war, or the hundreds of White supremacists who swarmed my city of Charlottesville, Virginia, in 2017, one driving a vehicle into a crowd of peaceful civil rights protesters, killing one person and physically and psychologically injuring others – a number too high to tally.

Our society is intrinsically racist.

Some of you reading this may balk, telling yourselves that we already know this about America and there's been deliberate ongoing work to eradicate the systems of racism pervasive in our culture.

If that is the case, then why is it that some people still refuse to believe they've benefitted from the pervasive foundation of White Supremacy?

One cannot align with movements advocating racial justice without acknowledging the disparities that permeate our nation.

I love America, and because I love it, I reserve the right to critique it. I reserve the right to expect that everyone who loves this country admit, on a fundamental level, the U.S. has historically perpetuated the notion that White people are superior. They must also admit that this philosophy is so ingrained in our social consciousness that some are willing to go to great lengths to preserve it.

We cannot — will not — move forward until we accept, recognize and develop a shared lens about our past, and accept that while we have made progress, White Supremacy is still a present-day reality.

We have a responsibility to advance racial equality for all people in our nation.

One cannot awaken without being honest with oneself. Just as a person addicted to a substance cannot become clean until they admit they have a problem; America must admit that it has a problem: White Supremacy and its byproducts of inequity and prejudice.

That. Is. The. Baseline.

.

Anger, Rage, and Pain

Accepting My Own Prejudice to Defeat White Supremacy in my Own Way

"Keep your money in your pocket, goddammit! If you walk around with your money out like that, them White folks will come and snatch it right out of your hand, hit you in the face, and there is nothing you can do about it. Do you hear me, boy? You think that you are special or that something is good about you walking around with that money out like that? You think that because you are a little boy them White folks won't snatch your little narrow ass up? Shit, you'll never see your little momma or pappy again."

I was six when my Great Uncle Wilbur, brother to my grandmother Evie Mae, spoke those words to me.

They're etched in my brain, a chilling reminder of the mechanisms of survival those who came before me had to employ to process and handle the racist-borne trauma inflicted on them.

My father's side of my family hails from Atlantic Beach, S.C., renowned as the "Black Pearl" of South Carolina's coastal region. The town's history is rich, overflowing with culture and character that harken to our Gullah heritage. It remains one of the only Black-owned beaches in the nation.

There, I learned the power of Black people working together. The businesses are Black-owned. The homes are Black-owned. The town is Black-owned.

My grandmother's house was the hangout spot for the entire community. She kept an open-door policy and welcomed all with open arms.

In that kind of environment, I learned how to love people you don't agree with. I spent time among Black business owners and entrepreneurs. I realized we didn't need anyone else to come and save us.

But Atlantic Beach also has a racist past.

It was the "Black beach" at a time that Jim Crow-fueled segregation mandated that Blacks and Whites could not patronize the same beach.

White people went to Myrtle Beach. Black people went to Atlantic Beach.

So great was the partitioning of people that a divider was placed in the ocean to ensure Black people would not cross into White waters, as if any race - or any one person, for that matter - can lay claim to an entire ocean.

It's within that context that Uncle Wilbur, who lived in Longs, South Carolina, told me another story that still reverberates in my head today.

When he was a teenager, he and two friends were walking in town, discussing what they'd do during the upcoming weekend, when one of the teenagers accidentally bumped into an older White man. The teen held a crisp dollar bill in his hand.

The White man snatched the dollar bill from the boy's grasp and pushed him to the ground. He scolded my uncle's friend, who responded in a way the White man deemed disrespectful.

I'm not sure what that response was - whether it was a look, talking back, or merely not having moved out of the way fast enough. Either way, according to Uncle Wilbur, the boy was corralled by other men, taken to a tree, and raised in an attempted lynching.

My uncle's friend nearly lost his life because he accidentally bumped into a man while expressing excitement about the weekend. Had it not been for the people who found him and cut him down, he would've perished.

Uncle Wilbur held onto this story all his life and found it necessary to share it with me even as Alzheimer's ravaged his memory.

When he told me that story, I sat and cried. That's all I could do; I didn't know how else to respond.

It was worse than any horror story I could've imagined, and it was true.

I told some family members about what Uncle Wilbur shared with me. Some laughed. Some said he was losing his mind and the anecdote wasn't true. Others pretended like it never happened. The damaging psychological effects of White Supremacy swaying them to forget and behave as if it didn't exist.

How my family responded to that story is an illustration of how Black people historically have coped with White Supremacy.

We crack jokes. We smile and say, "yes sir" and "no sir" in public only to internalize our feelings of ridicule and rejection at home. We're so traumatized by the blood-stained past that we have trouble embracing the concept of change and racial progress in a society where so many are invested in keeping the racial status quo.

My grandmother was afraid for me when I told her I'd be moving to Virginia. She reminded me that while things might be different there, Charlottesville was a city where the Confederacy once reigned supreme. It was a place where my life would be equated to that of a stray dog, perhaps even lower.

I told her things had changed.

But it was in Charlottesville that I came to grips with my own internal fear and anger. It was in this city, once the proud home of Thomas Jefferson, that I began to break the mental chains of White

Supremacy that bound me in my own mind.

In Charlottesville, I began to conquer, unspool and overcome my own biases. Here, I began to speak out for what's right. I faced consequences head-on. I sacrificed comfort. I recognized the clarion call of White Supremacy as it spewed from the mouths of the bigot and responded with my own trumpeted declaration of war.

Although understanding my biases began in Charlottesville, understanding my Blackness began years earlier.

In seventh grade, my teacher gifted me with a copy of "Uncle Tom's Cabin."

The book was so complex I needed CliffsNotes to understand it. Still, I was impressed with Uncle Tom's nobility and infuriated with how harshly Legree treated him to the point of ordering his overseers to kill Tom.

I began harboring feelings of animosity. I questioned how White people could be so treacherous, calloused, and downright evil.

As a young man, I watched "Malcolm X" repeatedly. I walked around the house, grocery store, church and park, saying, "I am Malcolm X," just like the children at the end of the movie.

Looking back, I now understand that as I developed an appreciation and pride for my people, I simultaneously reacted to the pain and hatred White people have levied against us for generations.

As James Baldwin famously said, "To be a Negro in this country and to be relatively conscious is to be in a rage almost all of the time."

The more Blackness I adopted, the more my anger toward bigotry developed. The more I became inspired to help my people, the more infuriated I became about White Supremacy.

In my teenage years, it became even more difficult to process these potent emotions.

I did further research as I got older to help me understand. I read an article about adolescent maturity and the brain. It was written by three prominent doctors and researchers; Sara B. Johnson, Ph.D., M.P.H, Robert W. Blum, M.D., Ph.D., and Jay N. Giedd, M.D. In it, I found very useful information.

Scientists have determined that the human brain does not fully develop until people – particularly young men - reach age 30: "In the last decade, a growing body of longitudinal neuroimaging research has demonstrated that adolescence is a period of continued brain growth and change, challenging long-standing assumptions that the brain was largely finished maturing by puberty."

Further:

"The frontal lobes, home to key components of the neural circuitry underlying 'executive functions' such as planning, working memory, and impulse control, are among the last areas of the brain to mature; they may not be fully developed until halfway through the third decade of life."

Given these facts, how can a teenager who is still developing mentally, physically, and emotionally be expected to deal with the trauma of being treated differently than others in society on the basis of skin color alone?

How does a young Black man healthily exist with exposure to videos of people who look like him being shot down in the street by the ones sworn to serve and protect?

How do young people, still growing, understand macro- and micro-aggressions? How do we expect people to be OK when they're told they must behave a certain way when dealing with law enforcement, or they could die?

For me, learning to navigate all these do's and don'ts was

overwhelming. I had to come to grips with the fact that I, too, suffered from racially charged trauma.

Shortly after I was elected to Charlottesville City Council at the age of 29, I determined that I – like each and every person - was responsible for finding the resolve within myself to stand for what's right. There are no excuses. Not anymore.

We each have an obligation to rail against systems and byproducts of systemic oppression and inequity. By the same token, we must be careful to keep our passion for change from feeding our human desire to hate.

Ever since taking a more vocal and visible stance against racism, I've received death threats. So have my children and family. I was confronted, excoriated, and targeted by people who wanted to break my spirit. They were hell bent on sapping away my courage.

Between 2016 and 2018, I underwent a series of emotional ups and downs that led me to a personal epiphany: while White Supremacy rears its ugliness in various ways, how I respond will make all the difference.

At various times in my life, how I felt about White people wasn't always positive, affirming, or healthy. My heart had been hardened by the atrocities my people experienced and it was tough for me to cope with the rage that burned inside my chest.

I was building, leading, and collaborating with coalitions of people of different backgrounds, but in my heart I still harbored resentment against Whites.

Deciding I'd rather go forward than backward, I went to therapy. There, I discovered that to be the best me I had to leverage my own trauma, not be consumed by it.

The only way I could do that, however, was by learning to be whole emotionally, physically, and intellectually. It's not an easy balance to strike, but it does underscore my commitment to never allowing what transpires around me to stop me from pursuing racial equity and justice.

I aim to take it a step further. I've challenged myself to love every human being, no matter who they are or what they believe. I've challenged myself to practice "radical love."

Dr. Cornel West told me in August 2017, "Wes, I can and will love every person who is on this earth, as we are all God's creatures and it's my duty to love. But just because I love the person doesn't mean that I have to love the sin that's within them."

This principle of radical love I've adopted, as fringe as it may sound, has helped me understand that people are most often who they are because of their own experiences.

It's not my job to change anyone. It's my job to be patient with people and impatient for progress.

I will use my power as a Black man to progressively work to effect the necessary change for racial equity and justice. It's the kindling I'll need to fuel my fight to dismantle White Supremacy by any means necessary.

Food for Thought

After digesting this chapter, I hope you've begun the work of identifying your own traumas, privileges, power, and abilities in the context of how White Supremacy has shaped our modern-day existence. This work doesn't come easy for anyone - Black or White. That is why I have added a series of discussion questions for you to ponder at the end of different chapters throughout this book. I hope they inspire you to begin exploring within yourself and with others about White Supremacy and how you can take a part in dismantling it, piece by piece.

Reflect on the moment you *really* recognized your race or ethnicity.

- How did you find out?
- Did you feel good?
- Did you feel empowered?
- Did you feel different from others?
- Were you disappointed?
- Were you ashamed?

Now, think about the first time you realized there were people treated differently than you based on the color of *their* skin. How did that make you feel?

2. DECONSTRUCTING WHITE PRIVILEGE IS NOT A SOLO JOB

For Whites and Blacks: Finding Courage

According to Merriam-Webster, the definition of courage is the ability to do something that frightens one. For a lot of people who are either White or Black in America, the topic of race is polarizing, exhausting, or frightening. The courage that it takes to address race in a meaningful way is a skill that very few people possess. In order to effectively do so, we must understand exactly who we are, and what role we play as individuals in the grand scheme of the social hierarchy of our environments. It is my belief that White Supremacy is the most damaging and challenging characteristic of America. It is the very fundamental principle that our nation was built on. White Supremacy is the tool that shaped and developed the norms of our country. Reckoning with and subsequently defeating White Supremacy is a shared task for all of us who truly want a more perfect union for generations to come. If this is to manifest and come to fruition, then we must be honest about who we are as a people. We must be honest with what we are as a nation. We must be clear that we have a White supremacist in the Oval Office. We must be clear that the 45th president of the United States of America has an administration that is adamant that our nation was best and is best when White Supremacy reigns supreme. To be honest, this isn't very different from other administrations, only that the current occupant is more blatant and overt with his desires than those before him.

If we know that we are a nation based on White Supremacy, then collectively we have to solve the problem. I am not one that believes that simply because White people created and benefit the most from White Supremacy that it is only up to them to dismantle it. Yes, White people have a significant role in all of this. Yes, some can argue that it is up to them to solve it since they started it, and the majority of White people who are benefactors and perpetuators of White Supremacy mainly listen to other White people while ignoring the voices of Black people who they consistently wound. I will never disagree with this notion, nor will I condemn those who believe in such. However, my position is a simple one. If we truly want things to get better, at a faster rate, then we are all going to have to pitch in.

I first received the revelation that Black and White people had to work together to change our country's landscape when I moved to Charlottesville in September 2009.

I was thrust into a new place that I, having been born and raised in the Deep South, considered the North. I figured things would be different. I thought I'd step into a melting pot of culture, people, and experiences.

Then came reality. Charlottesville was the exact opposite of all that.

Like many other American cities, Charlottesville had two races: White and Black. Like many other American cities, it had two socioeconomic classes: rich and poor. And like many other American cities, those categories were drawn on very similar lines.

But there *was* something different here. Before "White ally" began to trend on social media, White people in this city were interested in using their privilege to make their home a better place. Many didn't know where to start or what to do, but still, they felt it was important to at least try to do something.

While they were few in number, the amount of White people I encountered willing to make Charlottesville racially equitable was higher than what I had seen in other southern cities.

This gave me hope and inspired introspection.

I realized that if I wanted to defeat White Supremacy, I couldn't merely scrutinize my White compatriots. I had to look inside myself and explore my own biases and prejudices. Then, I had to ask how I, a Black Christian husband, father, and community leader, was complicit in upholding the tenets of White Supremacy.

That may seem like an oxymoron. How could I, a Black man, help fuel the very beliefs and practices I warred so avidly against?

But after exploring some of the deepest truths about White Supremacy, I learned it's not just about race.

To create the change that we want to see, we must first understand who we are as individuals. One of the largest misconceptions about race is that "all people" can be racist. While there are several think pieces and writings about this, the fact of the matter, regardless of how you write it, this isn't true. HuffPost (formerly Huffington Post) Columnist, Doyin Richards, wrote one of the best and most thorough explanations on the difference between Racism and Prejudice in 2019. In his article, he broke down a real-life scenario that I believe a lot of White people who are looking to move into the social awareness, social justice, and dismantling White Supremacy space are dealing with. The White people who want to do well but are still learning feel jolted when they are met with energy that they aren't quite ready for. His example also displays where a growing number of Black people in America are, quite frankly, a lot of us are tired of the bullshit, and just telling it how it is, regardless if it means that it's going to lead to your White tears.

From the HuffPost:

"As a White mom raising White kids in Middle America, I pride myself on being as conscious as possible when it comes to racism. I ensure my kids embrace differences and teach them not to be colorblind. But last week one of my co-workers (who is a Black man) told me I'll never understand what racism is like because I'm White, and I wasn't sure how to respond. Though I certainly wouldn't call this racism, I've had people of color treat me negatively because I'm White. What should I tell my co-worker if this comes up again?" — Jody in St. Louis

Doyin Richard's response was gold!

"The short answer: I agree with your co-worker. You'll never understand what racism is like.

For example, I'm a proud feminist, and I'm educated when it comes to women's issues, but there's a good reason I'm not out here saying I know what it's like to be pregnant. Because I'm a man and I have no effing clue what being pregnant is like! I'm sure it's uncomfortable and painful, but I'll never know because I haven't lived it. So I listen to my mom friends tell their pregnancy stories without *adding any "yeah, buts" or whataboutisms — because quite frankly, that's not my lane, and it never will be.*

Now, let's not confuse racism with prejudice. Prejudice is the belief that a person or a group of people are less than because of who they are. In other words, if a Black woman tells you not to bring your bland, raisin-infused potato salad to the cookout because "White folks think salt is the best way to season food," she's not being racist. She's displaying prejudice against you and people like you (and against your potato salad). Black people can be prejudiced as hell, just like any other group of people. As a matter of fact, I think all humans are prejudiced in one way or another. But just because a Black person hurt your feelings that one time doesn't mean you've experienced racism.

This is where I'm going to lose some of you: I don't believe that people of color can be racist in America.

Racism is completely different from prejudice because it's systemic, *as the -ism suffix connotes. I'd define racism as a political, economic, or social system in which a dominant race uses its power to oppress others of different races. Also, because I know people will pull a hamstring running to find a dictionary to look up the definition of racism, I'll provide it from Merriam-Webster. (It's not far off from mine.) Racism: Prejudice, discrimination, or antagonism directed against someone of a different race based on the belief that one's own race is superior.*

When you experience rudeness from Black people, remember that they will never have the power you do as a White person. They don't live in a country where the laws, norms and rules benefit them. White people — er, White men — *were running the show around here long before the ink on the Declaration of Independence was dry. That's not to say White people haven't experienced discrimination, but the way America is currently set up, there's nothing White people can't have. Want to join the rap game, play professional basketball, or participate in any Black-dominated activity? If you're good enough, you're in.*

It's not the same for people of color. For example, there are only three minority head coaches in the 32-team NFL — in which almost 70 percent of the players are Black. Hell, Texas Tech University recently fired a White guy for losing more games than he won as the head coach there, and a couple of months later, the NFL's Arizona Cardinals hired him to be their head coach. If you're going to tell me the reason for the NFL's lack of minority head coaches is that they're unqualified, I can't take you seriously. But that's only the tip of the iceberg. Racism is when people of color are locked up for decades for marijuana charges but a White Stanford University swimmer was sentenced to a measly six months in jail after being convicted of sexual assault.

Racism is when a Black man visits a daycare center and is told there is a six-month waiting list to get his daughter enrolled but his White female friend speaks to the same woman a few hours later on the same day to get her infant daughter in and is accepted. Yep, that happened to me. The fear of racism is what made me inform my neighbors that I was going to host

a bunch of loud 5-year-olds for my daughter's birthday party. I didn't do it because I'm a polite guy. I did it because I didn't want the cops to roll through, since I'm literally the only Black man on my block. I could go on all day.

So, when someone tells you that you will never understand what racism is like, Jody, you should rejoice, because racism is demoralizing, painful and exhausting. Take the word of a Black guy who has endured decades of this. For those thinking that I'm a playing the victim card, here, please note that I'm not interested in sympathy or handouts. I just want empathy and understanding. If you truly want to be an ally against racism, here's my advice: Talk less and listen more when around people of color. Don't be that White person who will inevitably fill my inbox or Twitter mentions with reasons that racism doesn't exist (White Supremacy is one a hell of a drug, man). Hear the stories of people of color and learn from them. Then when you see racism in your community, fight like hell to destroy it. Again, as a White person, you're way more powerful than we are in that regard.

24

Martin Luther King Jr. Day is approaching, and we still have a long way to go to achieve his dream of racial equality. One thing I know for sure? We'll never get there without the help of good White people."

Honestly, this sums it up perfectly. However, I think this example does not go into the intricate details as to why this is accurate. Next, you will read a guide of sorts, compartmentalized for White people and Black people. In this collective space, here is how we move forward individually.

Message to White People: White Tears Won't Save You

The truth of the matter is that a lot of people, people of color – Black folks, are angry and awakening. Angry at the fact that every time we open up our social media apps, we see another instance of either a police officer beating or shooting an unarmed African American. Every time we turn on the television there is another story of a group of teenagers holding down a young Black kid and beating them up, cutting off their hair, or doing something vile which echoes the treatment that our great-grandparents received. Every time we open up our social media, we witness someone White getting probation or a weekend in jail – a slap on the wrist – for a crime that we know someone who is Black had to go to prison for. Every time a White person says something like "President Obama set the country back 50 years during his presidency because he consistently talked about race" or "I didn't own any slaves, why am I being blamed for what my ancestors did?"

I'm not asking for pity. Your pity, your tears, your newfound self-awareness will not lead to a more equitable place, your actions will. Confining yourself to spaces which only one or two Black people frequent, befriending a handful of Black people in your otherwise majority White world, and reading "Between the World and Me" by Ta-Nehisi Coates won't actually do anything. You must understand the intricacies of White Supremacy and decide what you will do to dismantle it. I'll break it down to you.

1. Stop Crying Every Time You Are Confronted with Racism.

One thing that Black people in the year of our Lord 2020 are sick of are White tears. Yes, I am aware that for some of you it is very difficult to confront your own racism without crying. You've been living your entire life believing that you are a good person, you have told yourself that you want to help all people, you even give the young Black kid who plays with your kids a ride home every now and again. There is no way that you can be racist or participate in White Supremacy, right? Wrong. And when people who live with the institutional and systemic racism on a daily basis have the courage to tell you that the world that you live in benefits you because it was created for, run by, and sustained by White people for the betterment and empowerment of White people like you, don't cry. It's often one of the things that makes people turn off. It can feel like a ploy to appeal to people's heartstrings, to move the conversation from the issue at hand, inequity and race, and to you and your emotions. If it hurts you to come to grips with the fact that you, your parents, and other family members have benefited in any shape, form, or fashion due to their race, imagine being in the shoes of someone who was stopped and beaten by police officers because of their race, or someone with the exact same qualifications as their counterpart who was denied a job because of their race, or someone who had their children spoken to like a dog in their classroom by their teacher because of their race, or someone whose grandparents had their children snatched from their arms and sold as property because of their race?

So, do us all a favor. Plant these examples in your head. If you have hard emotions during your next conversation about race, do your best to not make the situation feel as if you are hijacking the moment with your emotions or call for attention. It only makes people want to stop working with you, which is the last thing that we need. Your power is in your privilege, use it well.

2. Don't say, "I don't see color, only people" or "There is only one race, the human race."

These phrases are phrases that have been in existence for generations. Here is the thing that a lot of people (specifically White people but not limited to them, because some Black people also believe the same foolishness) fail to take into account when they make statements like this. These phrases hide the fundamental and underlying truth that our nation was founded, built on, and sustained by racism, and its byproducts are what has allowed one group of people to thrive. Regardless of how much we want to believe that we are beyond thinking about and talking about race, it still matters. If it didn't, I wouldn't have been called a "nigger" at least once a week every week for the past three years since publicly taking a stance against racism in my community. If it didn't, premier colleges across the country would not only now have their first Black Student Body President, or only now acknowledge the work of the enslaved people who built their buildings. If it didn't, the collegiate athletic sports that generate the most revenue (basketball and football), where the majority of the players are Black, have the coaches who are overwhelmingly White.

It's why we have only had a handful of Black Supreme Court Justices, only one Black President, less than five Black governors, and less than 20 Black

United States Senators since Reconstruction. Look at the Fortune 500 companies on the Forbes list, and then look at how many of them have Black CEOs. These examples are not all by coincidence or by happenstance. It's not because Black people don't work hard enough. It's not because Black people don't study the same way in schools. It's not because Black people are troublemakers.

In 2014, African Americans constituted 2.3 million, or 34%, of the total 6.8 million incarcerated population. Black men are incarcerated at more than five times the rate of Whites. The imprisonment rate for African American women is twice that of White women. Nationwide, African American children represent 32% of children who are arrested, 42% of children who are detained, and 52% of children whose cases are judicially waived to criminal court. Although African Americans and members of the LatinX community make up approximately 32% of the US population, the comprised 56% of all incarcerated people in 2015. If Blacks and LatinX persons were incarcerated at the same rates as Whites, prison and jail populations would decline by almost 40%. [i]

For White people to believe that they can choose to not see color or lump all people into one demographic (the human race) is a privilege that you have that others do not. Use your privilege to not do more harm with such statements, but to understand that this is the reality for most Black people and people of color in America. Your genetic package allows you to navigate certain systems that others cannot.

Columnist Roni Faida had one of the best examples of such that I've seen as of late. In a column for the HuffPost in 2017, Faida wrote, "Maybe you are one of those people that really wouldn't mind. Maybe you truly believe that you absolutely don't care about the color of someone's skin. But answer me this, how many people of a different color have been to your house to eat? How many times have you broken bread in the home of a person of color? When you reach for the phone to call one of your dearest friends, are any of them a different hue than you?"

Every White person who is committed to doing the work of dismantling covert and overt racism, dismantling White Supremacy, or making our communities a more equitable needs to think about the questions that were posed. Are your relationships genuine ones? If so, great, let's keep it going. If not, the answer is simple. Do better. How? Challenge yourself to step outside of your comfort zone. Challenge yourself to listen intently to those who have different lived experiences, and then use your innate privilege to fight for what's right.

3. Please stop asking the same three Black people that you interact with on a regular basis to be your end-all be-all guide on everything Black People.

During the White supremacist attack in Charlottesville in August of 2017, a large majority of the people fighting back were White. All of these things are not by coincidence. I, for one, do not speak for all Black people, but I can say that based on my experiences, Black people in some cases from certain places across the country are very reluctant to speak candidly to White people about race, especially in communities where racism is deeply entrenched.

Understanding the complexities of race from a lens in which you are consistently facing micro-aggressions or forced to assimilate to simply survive, not be ostracized, or be perceived as a troublemaker for speaking out due to the fact that you are fewer in number is a dilemma that a lot of Black people across America have to deal with.

If I speak about how I really feel about race, I am going to make people uncomfortable, potentially lose my job, and maybe have to fight someone. If I just smile and pretend that I agree with what "they" are saying or just tell them that "I'm not really into politics" it will allow things to move along and not cause any trouble. I think back to the backlash that came my way after leading the effort to remove Confederate statues in Charlottesville. The death threats to myself and my family, the consistent need for security, the near loss of my job and livelihood, I literally had people try to take away everything that I had worked for, not just because of my position on the statues, but because I chose to speak up. I can't count how many Black people I encountered who have said things like, "Told you them people were going to break you down" or "Them White people ain't going to allow you to anything around here again," or "Man, them people doing a modern day lynching to you, Wes. They're sending a message to all of us. See, this why I just go on about my business because I don't have the patience." In all actuality, what a lot of Black people were conveying to me was why they were afraid to speak up. The thought of people making them potentially lose their job for speaking up was terrifying. The thought of having their families in danger was too great a risk. Having to stand up and face the very people who they've been told had all of the power to make their lives a living hell was a chance that they didn't want to take. Look at what they did to the person who was supposed to be a leader. If they could do all of this to Wes, they can do it to anyone. That's what they really were saying to me.

So, what happens when you, a White person with what they perceive as power, asks them a question about race? What often happens is survival mode kicks in. "I agree with you, those statues don't mean anything to me anyway," or "You're right, I don't know why people make such a big deal about race." Essentially, they are distancing themselves from any kind of confrontation in public or in front of the people who they perceive to have the power to make their lives a living hell.

White Person: "How do you feel about the stuff

going in Charlottesville?" "How do you feel about
the death of Michael Brown in Ferguson?" "How do
you feel about all of this talk about race all of the
time? I'm personally tired of it."

Black Person: "I agree with you." Or "I don't really
get into politics." "I agree with you, I wish we could
all just get along."

Again, this is often a defense mechanism and survival tactic. I know
this to be true, because in the confines of our safe spaces, the
sentiments that are shared with me and others, are the complete
opposite. "Those White people don't even understand how we feel,"
descriptions about how the conversations went, followed by listing
the things that we wished we had said, letting all of it loose in our
safe spaces and/or in private. Now imagine the inner toll that it takes
to live like this day in and day out. This is a small look into what it's
like to live a life without privilege.

Message to Black People: Finding Your Power, Using Your Power (Balance educating White people about our experiences and cussing them out)

There is an art to knowing how to develop an ally without making
White people jump off of a cliff with our approach. Don't get me
wrong: yes, some people need to get the raw and brutal truth to
understand the severity of the situation. However, in terms of
effectiveness, knowing when and where to say certain things can
make all the difference.

My brothers and sisters, I know some of you are reading this and upset
with me for sharing so many of our secrets or things that we
speak about behind closed doors. However, if they don't know,
we can't make things better. Now, we too are not without fault.
Nor is it as if we don't need to play a role in dismantling White
Supremacy. Often times, the ones that

we are looking to save us are someone else. There are excuses galore about why things are not working out in our collective favor due to an array of difficult circumstances created by people who view us as less than stray dogs.

One of the first things that I recommend for Black people is to truly learn and understand who we are in the United States of America. It's incredibly difficult to feel empowered when you do not know who you truly are. If we leave it to our local school systems, state education systems, or the federal government to teach us about who we are, then we many of us will continue to walk with blinders on about our own identity. With knowledge of self, with knowledge of culture, with knowledge of your people and your true self, empowerment will become second nature. I will never forget the feeling that I had at 9 years old watching the Malcolm X, the movie directed by Spike Lee. For months, I would walk around my apartment, the grocery store, my school, my neighborhood, and everywhere else saying the tagline from the end of the movie, "I Am Malcolm X." I am also very clear that I was fortunate. I grew up and was molded in Atlanta, Georgia, in the mid 1990s and early 2000s, an era that showed Atlanta to be the epicenter of Blackness, Black Pride, and cultural empowerment. I grew up seeing Black mayors, Black police chiefs, Black firefighters, Black educators and Black business owners, and believed without a shadow of a doubt that I could be whatever I wanted to be.

My father's side of the family derives from Atlantic Beach, South Carolina, also known as the "Black Pearl." Directly from the town website: "The rich culture of the town of Atlantic Beach was formed mostly of Gullah/Geechee people, descendants of slaves who lived for 300 years on the Sea Islands from Wilmington, North Carolina, to Jacksonville, Florida. In the early 1930's, defying Jim Crow laws in the segregated south, debunking Black stereotypes, and broadening the enterprises of the Gullah/Geechee people, Black men and women opened hotels, restaurants, night clubs, and novelty shops in Atlantic Beach."

In Atlantic Beach, I learned the power of our people working together. My grandmother Evie Mae Bellamy's house was the hangout house for the entire community. She always had an open door and welcomed all with open arms. It was here that I learned the power of community, working together, showing love to people that you didn't necessarily agree with, and most of all, that we (Black folk) didn't need anyone else to save us. We can and we will save ourselves. I grew up with this sense of pride. I grew up with this sense of belief. I grew up loving myself, loving us, and believing that the world was my oyster.

But what about the young Black person who didn't grow up in an environment that helped nurture that sense of Black Pride? I'm thinking of the person who was taught to believe that the Black Panthers were a terrorist group on par with the Ku Klux Klan, not that they cared about protecting, serving, and looking out for other Black people, because loving Black people is synonymous with hating White people. What about the Black adult who has been told all of their lives that Black people were inferior? The Black person who while matriculating through their elementary and middle school knew that they were smart, but was never tested to get into the "gifted" class? The Black person who loved to read and enjoyed math but was encouraged to stay in the classes with their friends, rather than being pushed up to honors-level classes? The Black person who had a parent or advocate push for them to enter the honors level, but when they got in there was met with so many micro-aggressions from their White peers that they played down on their intelligence so that they could return to classes where their friends were? What about the Black kid who at a very early age has a command of the English language, but is told "stop talking White" and it kills their confidence? What about the Black kid who has support, enters the higher-level classes, but once there, is told repeatedly by White classmates, "You aren't like other Black kids – you are more like one of us." What about the kid who actually comes to believe that they aren't like other Black kids at their school, in their neighborhoods, or in their families, and so develop a disdain for their own, and adopt racist ideologies themselves?

What about the Black kid who has parents who are determined to not allow their child to become a statistic so they isolate the child from all Blackness, tell them to not see color, place the child in private schools, and pray that this shields the child from the perils and ills of systemic oppression and White Supremacy... only to have that child called a nigger and a monkey in school, treated differently by the teachers, have their dreadlocks cut off as part of a "joke", or watch their White friends let off by the police while their child is detained during an encounter with law enforcement?

Unfortunately, these examples are all too common, all too real, all things that many of the Black people reading this will nod their head about when reading.

What do we do to empower those children and those families? Is there a magic wand that shields them from White Supremacy at a young age? Is there a special code that families can use to block White Supremacy? The answer is no. These issues are rooted in systems and institutions that have developed and been perpetuated over generations.

But the solutions are within us. All of us.

There is another component that we need to consider. We often think about White Supremacy in overt ways, but often leave out the byproducts of the systemic practices of White Supremacy that have led to a litany of different issues within all communities, and for the sake of this book, within many (though not all) Black communities. Who helps mentor the young man with dreadlocks who is 19 years old, who knows every Lil Boosie and NBA Youngboy record, who already has two felonies, who may wear his pants below his waist, and has two children? He wants to do better and is looking for help. Do we help him, or do we condemn his attitude and give up? Who helps the young woman who is 21 years old, has three children, didn't finish high school, lives in public housing, will "cuss" (not curse) "yo ass out", but really wants a better life? Do we say that she is too loud, too much, and we can't do anything with her, or do we utilize our skills as a village to help her? What

34

about the Black transwoman who was sexually abused at 9, ran away at 16, has been in a sex trafficking circle, and is now 25 and trying to figure out her life? Do we accept her and support her? Or do we follow an outdated tradition and say that her lifestyle is an abomination and turn her away? I'll be honest, I am not one of these folks who say that we have to pull ourselves up by our bootstraps, that if I did it, then you can too. But I do believe that our solutions can come entirely from our love and support of one another.

When we talk about empowering each other, we have to learn to love each other. In my opinion, in 2020, a lot of Black people are opening up our minds to understand the fact that we are not a monolithic group. White Supremacy has often led our older generations to believe that we had to be a certain way to be accepted by society and get ahead in life.

I will never forget the feeling that I had when I officially defended my dissertation and became "Dr. Wes Bellamy". Granted, it was the exact same weekend as the Unite the Right White supremacist attack on Charlottesville, but for a moment I was extremely proud to accomplish a goal that no one else in my family had achieved. However, after posting a picture on social media with my family and friends after my dissertation defense, I was soon met with comments calling me "Dr. Nigger Bellamy", or saying, "Who let this Nigger get a doctorate at their school?" The message was clear to me: no matter what we do, whether it's obtaining the highest levels of education, or wearing a suit and tie every day, or speaking a certain way, or making ourselves smaller to make other people feel bigger, in this society, many of us are going to be seen as what we have always been seen as in the eyes of people who look down on us. So, we don't have anyone to impress, prove anything to, or shine for, except for ourselves. As Black people in America, the only people that we have to concern ourselves with is ourselves. As individuals and collectively, from the year 1619 when the first enslaved Africans arrived in Virginia, we have had to navigate systems created by people who sat back and benefited from our

35

blood, sweat and tears. White supremacists and White Supremacy created many of the policies that we are currently forced to navigate through in education, economics, housing, politics, and our society as a whole. It would be foolish for me to say that we should ignore all of the rules that are currently in place, but as we matriculate through these systems, always remember to empower each other. Our job is not to assimilate but to matriculate and subsequently empower.

To empower each other does not mean to hate others. Let me reiterate this one more time, as undoubtedly, some will take my statements to be anti-White. Let me be clear: to be pro-Black or for Black people, to want to encourage, work for, love, and empower other Black people is not synonymous with being anti-White. The notion that Black empowerment is anti-White is another byproduct of White Supremacy. Members of different ethnic groups such as the Jewish community, the Irish community, people of Asian backgrounds, and so forth are rarely, if ever, questioned about being anti-White for their affinity for their ethnic group. White Supremacy is so prevalent that even some Black people believe that something is wrong with publicly declaring their affinity for each other, their support of each other, buying from their own businesses, loving each other, and overall simply enjoying each other. Many of our own have believed that we are lazy, that we don't work hard, that we don't want to do better for ourselves, that we are violent, that we are hyper-sexual beings, that we are careless with our money, that we don't love our children, that we don't love each other, and other painful, harmful, and vile stereotypes that people have started about us to psychologically keep us from using our collective energy to be the change that we want to see. I say, no more.

Black people in this country did more than just live through 250 years of slavery – we survived it. We didn't just live through 100 years of Jim Crow laws, Black codes, lynching, segregation, and racial terror – we survived it. But we are more than survivors: we thrive in any and every environment. So, there is no reason that we cannot dismantle White Supremacy and thrive as a people while doing it in 2020. Success for everyone looks different, as it is relative, but I am very proud of where we have come thus far, and where we are going in the future.

Food for Thought

After digesting this chapter, I hope you've begun the work of looking at why it's so important for us to work to dismantle White Supremacy. Here are a few questions for you to ponder after reading this chapter. For the questions below, I offer the following two definitions of prejudice and racism that might help you understand what it is we are trying to dismantle:

> **Prejudice** means making negative judgments about someone based on what they are, including race.

> **Racism** is prejudice plus power. Dr. Caleb Rosado (Department of Urban Studies, Eastern University, Philadelphia, PA) calls racism "the deliberate structuring of privilege by means of an objective, differential and unequal treatment of people, for the purpose of social advantage over scarce resources, resulting in an ideology of supremacy which justifies power of position by placing a negative meaning on perceived or actual biological/cultural differences." **(The Undergirding Factor is POWER Toward an Understanding of Prejudice and Racism)**

For White people who are reading:

Take a moment to reflect on the difference between racism and prejudice.

Do you agree with the assessment of racism and prejudice?

- Do you feel like you fit under either category of racist or prejudice?
- Do you feel as if you have tough conversations about race with your Black friends?
- Do you believe that they are being truthful with you?
- Do you assume they are right in how they perceive race?
- What is your role in dismantling White Supremacy?

For Black people or people of color who are reading:

Take a moment to reflect on the difference between racism and prejudice. Do you agree with the assessment of racism and prejudice?

- Have you ever been prejudiced towards a White person?
- If you have been prejudiced towards a White person, did it make you feel empowered?
- Do you feel as if you have tough conversations about race with your White friends?
- Do you believe that they are being truthful with you?
- What is your role in dismantling White Supremacy?

3. WE NEED TO HAVE A DIALOGUE – BUT WHAT IF I AM TIRED OF TALKING?

The day after a gunman killed 49 people and wounded 53 others in a spray of bullets at the Pulse nightclub in Orlando in the summer of 2016, I posted on social media a picture of me with a member of the LGBTQ+ community as we marched together in Charlottesville.

One of my closest friends, who had undoubtedly seen the photo in his social media feed, texted me, joking that I was a "faggot" for being with other "faggots and weirdos."

His words cut deep.

I immediately challenged him to a fight, and we had a lively discussion.

Two of my closest friends in Charlottesville at the time were Amy Sarah Marshall and Lisa Green, a gay couple who helped lead the Charlottesville Pride community. Knowing someone had used those hateful words in reference to two people I cared for was akin to someone calling one of my Black friends a nigger.

I wasn't going to tolerate it.

That was Wes in 2016. I hadn't always been willing to take that stance.

Like many other young Black men, I grew up in environments that preached that to be homosexual was to be judged, criticized, and in essence, dehumanized.

The prevailing idea was that men who loved men were weak, deviant, and weird. Although I had family members who were gay and generally did not care what people did in the confines of their own bedroom, I *did* tolerate – and repeat - gay jokes.

Even if I said they were lighthearted and harmless - even if I wasn't the one telling them - I was an active participant. It took time and work to mentally unravel the toxic masculinity and homophobia I had internalized.

In reference to the Black community in particular, writer and activist George Johnson is quoted telling gay lifestyle magazine *Queerty* that, "We have been conditioned by White Supremacy and patriarchy to act the way we do towards the LGBTQ community. It was passed down and through Black folk trying to 'get in' with [the] White community [and] they adopted many of the oppressive behaviors towards their own. So, this is something we must unlearn together as a community. We can't have conditions on Blackness, and Blackness can't exist without queerness."

As I became more immersed in the work of attacking White Supremacy, I realized something profound: one cannot believe in dismantling White Supremacy and be homophobic.

That's because homophobia, like racial prejudice, discrimination, and racially motivated hate crimes, is a byproduct of White Supremacy. The two are inextricably linked.

In May 2019, Hugh Ryan, author of "When Brooklyn Was Queer," penned a column in *The Washington Post* exploring the interconnectedness between homophobia and White Supremacy.

He writes, in part:

Anti-gay sentiments are usually traced to misogyny, fear of gender transgression, toxic masculinity and hidebound religious teachings. But one important factor regularly goes unacknowledged, curiously so, considering how often it comes up these days in other contexts: White Supremacy.

In the early 20th century, leading White American intellectuals embraced the pseudoscience of eugenics, which held that human beings were the sum of inherited traits that could be read by looking at someone's body. The fullness of your lips, for instance, might indicate how decisive you were, or the swelling of breast tissue on a man (a condition called gynecomastia) might be a tell-tale sign of criminality. Eugenicists believed those moral and physical traits were inseparable, and that children inherited them in direct and simplistic ways, like eye color. Therefore, the answer to all of society's ills lay in controlling human reproduction: in breeding our way to a brighter future.

Eugenics was largely a response to the expanded political, social and geographical integration of Black people in America, and those who practiced it were interested in protecting and perfecting "the White race." These were men like R. W. Shufeldt, a noted doctor with the U.S. Army and a prolific author of eugenic treatises.

In his 1915 book "America's Greatest Problem: The Negro," Shufeldt argued that Black women sought out White men because of their superior genes. ... This was a follow-up to his 1907 book, "The Negro: A Menace to American Civilization," in which he wrote that a Black man is "ready at any and at all times to do his share in debasing the blood of the White race in America."

To protect Whiteness, eugenicists like Shufeldt fought for bans on interracial marriage, tighter medical control over marriage licenses, increased power for the state to sterilize imprisoned people and increased regulations on prostitution, which they saw as a zone of possible race-mixing.

At the same time Shufeldt was writing about race, he was also researching a seemingly different topic: the defining of queerness, which he variously referred to as "passive pederasty," "inversion," "perversion" and "homosexuality."

As a eugenicist, Shufeldt didn't believe that someone's sexual nature could be changed, because he believed it was hardwired into the body (a more sinister ancestor to our modern idea of being "born this way"). But he did believe we could prevent queer people, in much the same way we could prevent racial miscegenation: by closely policing heterosexuality.

As he wrote in a 1905 paper entitled "The Medico-Legal Consideration of Perverts and Inverts," he believed that America "will continue to breed millions of sexual perverts and inverts — psychopathic types — just so long as any ignorant priest, justice of the peace or other party, is permitted to give people permission to breed them."

While this might seem far afield from his writings on race, it was really just the other side of the same eugenics coin: another effort to protect the White race through controlled breeding. To Shufeldt, Black people represented an external threat to Whiteness, and queer people represented an internal one (the existence of Black queer people seems never to have entered his mind). These were discrete issues, but they were both, at heart, about promoting White Supremacy.

I realized that if I wanted to dismantle White Supremacy, I had to dismantle my own homophobia as well.

I had always believed it was hypocritical for people who looked like me and had endured generational oppression for simply being who they were born to be make disparaging remarks about members of the LGBTQ+ community and treat them with contempt. But here I was, subconsciously and consciously supporting a system of hatred that belittled gay, trans, and Black people alike.

Today, I consider myself a staunch ally of the LGBTQ+ community. I stand beside my brothers and sisters, and those who refuse to take on a label in their fight for equality and fair representation.

I acknowledge my past as a hindrance to progress and seek to make amends by continually deconstructing my innate bias.

While learning about the different types of sexuality, I also had to come to grips with the fact that I am more than just what is inside of my pants. Historically, from the earliest days of this nation, Black men and women were viewed as hypersexual beings. The subjugation of the enslaved has been well documented, as many were forced by white people to do horrible things sexually in order to survive. I truly believe that subconsciously, this was, and still is, one of the factors that lead many Black men to equating their masculinity with their sexuality. While growing up, I remember hearing references to a man's worth being in direct correlation to the size of his penis. In order to be the best version of myself, this way of thinking had to be addressed internally, and rerouted in my actions externally. I am a work in progress, but I can truly say that therapy saved my life.

I believe it's impossible to destroy White Supremacy without destroying the hate we each carry within. It's OK to admit we're not perfect. It's not OK to refuse to do the work to become better.

That level of self-realization is an essential step to eliminating White Supremacy, which flourishes in what Michelle Alexander, author of "The New Jim Crow," calls the "racial caste system."

White Supremacy looks to create hierarchies in every arena.

People who are dirt poor, living on the lower rungs of poverty with no education, no job, no power, will still debase people who are gay.

In America, for White Supremacy to survive, there must always be some kind of hierarchy. It only exists and works well if one person is above the other.

Take slavery for example.

Even after being ripped away from their homeland, stripped of their culture and identities and forced to work under the most brutal of circumstances, some Black people believed they were better than others based on simple physical traits, such as the hue of their skin, the texture of their hair, or the color of their eyes.

White Supremacy created psychological schisms between enslaved people. Although they were all in the same dire situation, laboring under the same untenable duress, some were prevented from finding common cause with their brothers and sisters because they believed they were superior to the rest, thanks to separation by skin pigmentation, an outcropping of White Supremacy during the height of slavery.

America did similar things to different ethnic groups, including the Jews, Irish, Italians, and Japanese.

To be anything different than what White supremacists considered "pure White" meant something was wrong with you.

Being pure White became synonymous with being Christian, heterosexual, and stereotypically masculine or feminine. The mind control and categorization of people based on attributes that are White-adjacent or White-averse have worked so well that White people are not the only ones who perpetuate White Supremacy.

If White people, Black People, and everyone between truly want to defeat White supremacy, then we have to be honest with ourselves about who we really are as individuals. We have to be honest with ourselves about our conscious and subconscious biases. We have to be willing to fight the internal urge to tell ourselves that nothing is wrong with us, and push back against our brains when we begin to tell ourselves that we are not the problem. That internal work is beyond challenging, but necessary in this fight. As we travel down the road to self-improvement and shredding our biases, we have to be willing to listen, learn, dialogue, and then act.

According to Merriam-Webster's dictionary, the definition of the word *dialogue* is a simple one: "a conversation between two or more persons." The definition of the word *act* is "the doing of a thing." In today's society, in nearly every city, in nearly every state, regardless of what people look like, who they vote for, who they choose to love, or how much money they make, people can benefit from *talking* about their differences. Communication is one of the fundamental principles of human interaction. However, when it comes to matters pertaining to race, more often than not, the conversations can be more polarizing than any other subject. The reason is that a lot of people are simply not used to talking about the topic with people who are different than themselves. Some people fear that they will say the wrong thing. Some people don't want to be blamed for what their ancestors did in years past. Some people don't want to be blamed for the traditions that their grandparents and parents passed down to them. Some people just don't like confrontation at all, so they avoid the topic at all costs. Other people have been conditioned to not talk about certain things around certain people. Other people believe that nothing will change by talking. Other people believe that it's too frustrating to speak to people who don't get it, so why try? Some of these same people are also not educated on race relations. Some believe that they have been dealt a bad hand and they just have to make the best of it. Some believe that race isn't really a factor, and with hard work, they can accomplish whatever it is that they set their minds to. I guess what's clear amongst everything is that people are complicated and trying to get all of these different kinds of people on the same page can require Herculean effort. But if we don't fight to come to the table to have the difficult dialogue and follow through with tangible action items, then we as a society will never reach our full potential. Personally, I believe that the majority of people in our society want better, and because of this, we have to do more than talk. I firmly believe that we have to act!

On March 22, 2016, I stood looking at nearly 100 people with Confederate flags, signs with people calling me all kinds of *nigger*, and people saying directly that I was causing strife within our community. It was on this date that my City Council colleague Kristin Szakos and I, along with several other members of the community, hosted a press conference to announce that we, as two city councilors, would be pursuing an effort to have the City of Charlottesville remove the statue of Confederate general Robert E. Lee from a downtown park. There had been a great deal of dialogue, discussions, forums, and other forms of talking about race, the statues specifically, and the need for change within the city prior to that March press conference, but for some people, this event felt like it was literally going to tear the community apart. From the local paper, the Daily Progress:

"The proposal was met with resistance Tuesday as Confederate heritage and preservation groups such as the Virginia Flaggers and Army of Northern Virginia-Mechanized Cavalry protested the conference.

... Arriving shortly before the start of the news conference, Robert Lee Elliott, of Albemarle County, carried a sign that referenced Bellamy as a "trouble maker."

"I believe in the South and what it represents. It's country folk and living." Elliott said. *"I hate to see history being changed. ... History is in the past and we need let things lie the way it is."*

"The more you stir the pot, the worse it stinks. It's getting a lot of people upset," he said. *"If someone doesn't like the name Lee Park or doesn't want to go through it, that's their priority. I don't like going to the Downtown Mall after dark, so I don't do that."*

Several protesters Tuesday said Bellamy and the rest of the council are guilty of promoting strife.

"This was a rigged job," said Joe Draego, a protester who repeatedly interrupted speakers during the conference.

As Draego yelled at the speakers, he questioned whether anyone with an opposing view would be allowed to speak at the event. Bellamy said everyone would eventually have an opportunity to weigh in on the debate, but none of the protesters were invited to speak Tuesday.

"There should have been an opposing point of view. When people can't have an opposing point of view or a respectful conversation, that's all that's left — hollering over speakers because we can't speak ourselves," Draego said.

"Wes Bellamy is creating divisiveness and hatred, not unity," he said.

"By tearing this statue down and allowing gay activists, the NAACP and the Black Lives Matter groups to use it for their agenda, the City Council is dividing our nation once again and erasing all the work Lee did over 150 years ago," the petition says."

It was clear on this day in March that the topic of race was one that some members of our community had a lot of issues with. However, it further played out in the coming months about exactly how much we as a society needed to do in order to get to a better place.

Let me be clear with a few things. The following does not exclude you from being racist or prejudiced:

- ☐ Having a Black friend
- ☐ Having an interracial relationship
- ☐ Having a biracial grandchild, niece, nephew, cousin, or any other family member

- ☐ Being nice to the one or two Black people that you have had to interact with at work
- ☐ Having pity on someone of another race and helping them out because you feel sorry for them
- ☐ Voting for Wes Bellamy in a city council race
- ☐ Donating to a cause that helps marginalized communities
- ☐ Voting for President Obama
- ☐ Voting for Black Republicans or Independents

I can't explain how many times I was told over the next 12 months, and still to this day if I am being honest, about how people contend that they can't be racist or prejudiced because they did one of the aforementioned actions. The sacrifice for pushing towards a more equitable society is one that requires a great deal of work, and it's the kind of work that makes us question our deepest and internal thoughts. Think about it: if defeating White Supremacy was easy, then why is it still so prevalent? This work is challenging, but it can be done. We just have to ask ourselves, what are we willing to sacrifice? Are we *only* going to talk about it, or are we going to *act?*

Message to Black and White people:

I will be honest. One of the most frustrating phrases that I have heard on a much more consistent basis the past few years is "We need to have a dialogue." As the occupant of the White House has emboldened White supremacists, White nationalists, and domestic terrorists, the calls for civil discussions have increased from people on all sides of the political and social spectrum. There appears to be a thought amongst some people within our nation that if people were to just get into a circle and share their experiences about race, then race relations would dissolve within the Great United States. The reality is that for a lot of Black people in America, the time for talking has come, come around again, left, came back, and is brought up again during moments of racial strife within local communities, statewide initiatives, and national crises, only to die

48

after the initial conversations end. It often feels as if the "dialogue" is mainly for White people, as Black people have been living with these issues for hundreds of years. For better or worse, we have learned to survive and navigate the political and social climate no matter who's in office or what national tragedy takes place. The question then becomes what can both Black and White people do collectively in order to bring about some form of actual reconciliation. I do believe that we must consistently and persistently push for unity, but understand that there can be no reconciliation without the reallocation of resources – at the local, state, and federal level – to Black people for building this nation for free. One thing that is clear, the United States of America was literally founded and built on racism, racist practices and policies, and for centuries has made excuses about why race relations have not improved and could not improve, and/or lied about the rate of improvement. In order for any of us to have any kind of reconciliation, we must be honest with each other, be brutally honest with each other, and be prepared to do the work *after* the dialogues.

The summer of 2020 saw protests galore, even in the midst of a pandemic. People of all races are tired of the status quo, want things to change, but are not sure what to do beyond the protest. However, there are distinct differences in what we see on television and social media pertaining to massive protests in the streets, and every day places in America where progression is as slow as the dial up internet at my grandmothers' house when all of my cousins were over. In those communities, dialogue is still believed to be somewhat taboo. Talking about empowering Black people is often placed in the same boat as people pushing for a race war, and things would all be better if we just prayed for each other, went to church, and sang hymns. In many places across America, talking about the issues in the community pertaining to racial strife is better off just left alone, because as they say, "talking about this stuff just stirs stuff up." Well….that is unless the conversations take

place on social media. Social media in small towns, medium sized cities, and large metropolitan areas alike can be dynamite or connectors for social unity.

Who stands with the people pushing for change in the places where there aren't any cameras, their rally can cost them their livelihood, and the number of people willing to be bold and speak out our few? These are the places where White people have to be willing to use their social capital – it is here where they must use the privilege that will shield them from the job loss, the housing loss, the livelihood damage that people of color face for speaking up. It is also in these places where Black people have to rally together and use their collective power. It is these places where our voices must be strong. Where our strength must be in our numbers. It is here where we must call on the ancestors, where we must agree that we don't have to do everything the exact same way, where we fight White supremacy as a balled fist oppose to an individual finger.

In the year 2020 we have seen nearly every major media outlet declare that Black Lives Matter. We have seen nearly every major sport declare that Black Lives Matter. We have seen politicians, athletes, entertainers, teachers, members of the military, commercials, boycotts, and campaigns all follow suit with the declaration of *Black Lives Matter*. However, we have also seen towns, cities, counties, and municipalities as a whole move in the opposite direction. This there in itself describes the complexity of our nation. Many people find themselves frustrated and feeling as if, "If we just could have a conversation with each other, we could hear each other. Our hearts may change if we begin to understand each other." I am sorry to be the bearer of bad news, but conversations and dialogue about conversations don't improve race relations. Actions, policy change, resource reallocation, redistribution of power, and a commitment to being uncomfortable is what moves the proverbial needle. I am always happy to talk, but I find solace in knowing that we are acting!

Finding the Common Ground –

We can concede the fact that we live in a nation built on White Supremacy, while still respecting and loving each other. I have been a part of several "dialogues" about race relations. Roundtable discussions brought together people of different backgrounds to discuss their feelings, different ways to move forward as a people, and were more or less a waste of time. These discussions, often majority White, touched on root causes, discussed current issues, had people listen and ask questions, but in my opinion, once the discussions were over, that was it. However, I have been a part of a few discussions that were powerful. In my experience, the best discussions of race all ended with a simple question for all parties involved: "Now that we have had this discussion, what are you willing to give up?" "Now that this discussion is over, what are you willing to sacrifice?"

Message White people:

For White people, what part of your privilege are you willing to give up? What part of your life are you willing to sacrifice for the greater good of race relations? These questions are often the ones that lead people to get to the root of how they truly feel. Whether your family was extremely affluent, middle class, working class, or poor, to be White in America is to be privileged. This fact is one that makes a lot of people uncomfortable. Following this fact up with a question about what one is willing to give for others reveals how truly ready a person or community is for real reconciliation.

If one recalls the White Supremacist attacks in Charlottesville, it was mostly White people from our communities fighting off the neo-Nazis. They were willing to risk their safety to stand up against White Supremacy. Are you willing to sacrifice your comfort – the comfort of being able to live in a world where you can be race neutral? The comfort of telling yourself and your children that everyone has the same opportunities, while ignoring the inequity in our criminal justice system, in our financial industries, and our day to day lives? Are you willing to sacrifice and interrupt your life as you know it to be an ally, to do the necessary work of educating yourself on the history of our nation, the work of undoing your racial bias, and having the courage to speak up once you know better? It is difficult, for sure, and for some this is a radical shift, but if we want our dialogue to not be in vain, the aforementioned is necessary.

Message to Black people:

Every Black person in the United States of America has to be willing to answer a fundamental question if we are going to move forward collectively as a nation. We have to ask ourselves what we are willing to sacrifice? Being open to new encounters with people is a challenge in itself. Our own internal bias and outright skepticism has become a defense mechanism of sorts, but in order for this country to move forward, we too have to do our part. Many will say that we have done more than enough by sacrificing our bodies, our children, our wealth, our sanity, our everything for a society that sees us as little more than livestock. I distinctly remember watching my grandmother, Evie Mae Bellamy of Atlantic Beach, South Carolina, working for a White family, the Upchurches, who owned a local restaurant in which she loyally worked, served, and cleaned up. She also (was the family's resident babysitter, essentially helping raise several of the Upchurch children to adulthood. They came to love and accept my grandmother as a member of their family, and I have always marveled at the affection that she had for them. On the surface, one may believe that this is part of what's needed for the improvement of race relations. A White family in the deep South loving a Black woman as their own.

However, I will also never forget a cousin of mine being at school, having an interaction with one of the Upchurch children, and the child making the remark, "His grandma is my family's maid. She's kind of like our in-house slave. She washes our clothes and folds them, cooks for us, and does whatever we tell her to." I'll never forget the look on my cousin's face as he retold that story. I also think about the sacrifice that my grandmother made. Sacrificing time with her own family to take care of someone else's. Taking on the ridicule of others for what she believed to be the betterment of her family. This sacrifice was not in vain, but it makes me think it was worth it. In her eyes, it was. My initial thoughts while growing up with this level of resentment for that family was that Black folk in America have to stop sacrificing ourselves and become selfish: selfish in regard to continuing to build up our families and our own communities. We must refuse to sacrifice our social and emotional capital only to make other people comfortable. Some reading may ask where is the common ground in for all in Black people being selfish with putting themselves first? To that point, we must be willing to effectively communicate to our White brothers and sisters why it is important for us to get our own house in order before we can do anything else. The common ground comes in the communication of why this is necessary. The common ground comes in the need for consistent round tables and circles of dialogues about race relations, regardless of how exhausting and fruitless that they may initially seem. The fact of the matter remains that in order for people to grow, they must be first open to learning, educated and exposed to different cultures, and then *act* by incorporating the lessons learned in their day-to-day lives. The path forward requires sacrifice in comfort levels for Black people to be open and willing to look past the transgressions of the country, and deal with the individual healing of our communities.

The sacrifice comes in the need for some Black people to stop assimilating with the majority and being willing to love and help each other. The sacrifice for some Black people to also do the internal work of undoing the brainwashing of their local schools and communities in terms of believing that "White is right" and truly understanding that you are good enough by your own standards. The sacrifice of not looking down on other Black people who may be different from you, but still deserve and are worthy of your collective love and support. My brother, my sister, my non-gender identifying family member, you are good enough. Because you are good enough, you don't have to make a joke about our people in front of White people to cut the tension and/or break the ice. You don't have to speak down on Black owned businesses with poor customer service and writing all of them off while simultaneously frequenting businesses who see you as no more than a dollar sign. The sacrifice of undoing the programming that has taught you to think negatively about your own but empowering those who look like you. The sacrifice of understanding that to love your own does not mean that you hate others. The sacrifice of being selfish enough to love yourself first, and open enough to be committed to doing the difficult work of helping others learn to love us as well. It's not fair. We shouldn't have to do it. We have sacrificed enough, and there are several other reasons that we can find to not hang in there and educate our White brothers and sisters on why this work is needed, but the fact remains that if we take an adversarial approach in every situation things will never get better.

To this point, before we can be patient with others, before we can lead others, before we can truly engage in this transformation dialogue revolving around race, we have to be willing to educate and help ourselves. We are all aware of the fact that we cannot rely on our public, private, or charter school systems to educate our children on our history. Our history didn't begin with enslaved Africans, nor does it end with Barack Obama becoming the President of the United States. It is imperative that we educate ourselves on the work of Mansa Musa of Mali, the truth work of the Black Panthers and their 10-point program, the value of supporting Black transwomen, and understanding just how powerful we are as a collective. Dr. King's infamous speech, "I am Black and Proud" speaks to how nobody else can do this work for us. If this is true, then we must be patient with each other and impatient with progress. Allow each other grace and mercy, while educating each other. Love and support each other while taking care of each other. In order for all of this to come to fruition, we must commit ourselves to having dialogue amongst ourselves. These discussions require patience. As hard and challenging it is to speak to White people and other ethnic groups about the struggles and needs of our people, it can be even more challenging to do so with our own. Let's be clear, having a disagreement does not mean that we are divided, in fact, it simply means that we are not a monolithic group that has to always agree. We can disagree without being disagreeable and hurtful. We can have different vantage points and perspectives on liberation and empowerment without believing that one person is right or wrong. We can work together, work in silos, or collaborate only when necessary, and not have to feel as if this group or that group is not committed to the cause. The notion that we all have to do the exact same thing, view things the exact same way, or be aligned in one particular manner on any situation is a concept that has bestowed upon us by the oppressor. I can point to cultures of people from across the globe who do not operate from a monolithic viewpoint or perspective, and do not receive the same backlash that Black people do for working in our own way. Do not subscribe to this notion. Remain diligent, remain persistent, remain open minded, and most of all, keep the collective energy in mind in everything that we do. In order to do so, we must sacrifice our thoughts of negativity towards each other. The dialogue is and work together is possible. We just have to do it.

4. THE PRIVILEGE TO FIGHT

What many people fail to understand is the cost that one has to pay for fighting for what is right. Have you ever thought about what it costs you to fight? Fighting for rights, fighting for your marriage or relationship, fighting for what you believe in, fighting for your children, your siblings, your parents, your friends, physical or mental. How much does any of this cost?

In many ways, the ability to be a freedom fighter is a privilege. According to the Oxford dictionary, a privilege is a special advantage not enjoyed by everyone. Privilege comes from the Latin word *privilegium*, meaning a law for just one person, and means a benefit enjoyed by an individual or group beyond what is available to others.

I will never forget having a conversation in a church in Charlottesville in early 2019. There was a buzz around the city, and it felt as if everyone and their mother was asking me in one way or another if I was going to run for re-election to the Charlottesville City Council. To be honest, the four years had taken a toll on my marriage, my relationships with my children, my mental health, and even my physical health. I was on the fence, to say the least. I knew that I provided a voice for a lot of people and spoke in ways that made a lot of people feel represented. We had done some incredible work during my time on Council, and I was proud to have served. I gained a ton of experience and grew as a person during those four years, and honestly felt that it was time for someone else to take the baton. For the first time in our city's history, we had two African Americans serving on the Council at the same time (myself and Mayor Nikuyah Walker). However, as I sat in the pews of this particular historically Black church that was filled to the brim with folks discussing issues and matters within the city, I noticed that there was no one in the audience who was thinking about filling my seat. As the questions continued to come about where I thought the city was going, and the things that I was working on, I asked a question back to the crowd, "Why aren't any of you thinking about running for office?" We have had fewer than ten Black people in the history of the city on city council. Why is that? The responses that I received were disheartening, but not surprising. "We saw the Hell they put you through; why would anyone in their right mind want to go through that?" I was also told, "Wes, you learned something that a lot of us from here already knew. These White folks don't want to see any of us get too big for ourselves. The moment that they start to think that you are going to change something, they will use everything that they can to destroy you. You know that."

This conversation reminded me a great deal of one that I had in the winter of 2016 with former Charlottesville vice-mayor and the beloved mother of the community, Dr. Holly Marie Edwards. I was immersed in what I considered to be one of the most troubling times of my life, as I was under attack from White supremacists for pushing for the removal of the statue of Confederate general Robert E. Lee from a city park. I had started receiving phone calls during the Thanksgiving holiday break, shortly after the Presidential election, being told that "This is Trump's country now, you nigger." "We are going to break your Black ass down to your knees and take away every position you have." Lo and behold, they tried it. The ringleader, Jason Kessler, had just discovered and published a series of homophobic, immature, and flat out unacceptable tweets I had posted when I was in college and shortly after I graduated. He and his followers were adamant that I was not fit for office or any position of leadership due to these thoughtless posts. When my colleagues on Council all stated that they had seen me grow up over the years, and believed that the tweets didn't reflect who I was today, Kessler's crew took me to court to try to have me removed from office, dragging the saga out in the media, and eventually losing. They pressured the Albemarle County School Board to remove me as a teacher (I resigned to protect my students from the hate campaign). Eventually, this same group called the

KKK   to come to the city on my one-year wedding anniversary and ultimately held the Unite the Right Rally that brought so much pain to the city. They wanted to intimidate me and anyone else who was watching.

Holly was the last African American to serve on the city council prior to me being elected. She and I both cried during the chat, as she made it clear that what was happening to me was not just about me. The people behind this were trying to send a clear message to all of us. "Stay in your place, or we will take everything away from you." Looking back on the events, I won't say that they were successful, but they definitely made their point. When you speak up and speak out, specifically to matters revolving around race, you become a target. You run the risk of losing your job, being threatened, and your life becomes very uncomfortable.

I have been in Charlottesville for ten years, and the city has provided me with an education about fighting for what's right like no other. I also have had the privilege of traveling the country and the world, discussing equity and justice. Unfortunately, in most cities, states, and continents, the sentiments are the same. Fighting for what's right is a privilege, and it's one that a lot of Black people and people of color in majority White landscapes don't have. The courage to fight for what you believe in requires you to feel empowered – to feel that you have the power to be able to speak out and be effective.

One thing that I have noticed throughout my travels over the past few years, and while I look back on history, feeling of empowerment that often leads to people speaking up favors the already privileged. Even when some localities have higher numbers of Blacks than Whites, tradition and the fear of what *may* happen if Blacks "stir up too much trouble" makes a lot of people not want to get civically engaged.

There have been occasions in which Black people speak up and push for more, but they are almost always met with an incredible amount of pushback. Historically, the most progress has been made when Black people speak up as a group, and our White allies have the courage to stand up beside/behind us.

Some privilege can be gained through other means than White *allyship*, though. When *some* Black folk are able to articulate their positions in a way that surprises White people, it can provide them with the opportunity to enter and navigate certain social settings. When they attend certain colleges, join certain fraternities or sororities, join certain social clubs, begin to gain wealth, and obtain certain political or social positions, they are afforded access to a certain level of privilege.

The feeling of *knowing and believing* that you are entitled to certain inalienable rights is different from *hoping* that you are going to be treated fairly. This privilege goes hand-in-hand with a feeling of empowerment. Unfortunately, the number of Black people who indeed know this invigorating feeling are few and far between. There is often an unspoken word amongst our society, especially for Black people, that the people who are "allowed" to feel empowered are a select few. W.E.B. DuBois insisted that this was the Talented Tenth. Others call it the chosen ones. Some simply write it off that certain people are meant to be leaders, and others are meant to be followers. However, what has actually transpired is that since the days of enslavement, Blacks have been told that only a few of us are good enough. Only certain ones of us were allowed to work in the house. Only a certain caliber of negro was allowed to be showcased and not subjected to the cruelties of others. Only a certain kind of Black person was permitted to speak up for the people. Only a certain kind of Black person was to be followed by the masses. Only one Black person can get that coveted job in the company. Only one Black principal for an entire school division. Only one Black elected official at a time. Only one who knew how to dress well, speak well, played the game well, or was "special." I remember being told that I was special when I was five years old, and actually believing it. It essentially is what separated me and some of my friends who were eventually incarcerated or murdered due to their lifestyles. I vividly remember being on different programs with people I knew, and they would say things like "I may not speak as well as Wes Bellamy, but I will try my best." We, Black people, even in the year 2020, have bought into the notion that privilege is only for a few, that empowerment is only for the called, that defying the odds is only for the select. However, imagine what society would be like if we *ALL* believed that we have the unalienable right to life, liberty, and the pursuit of happiness. What would happen over the next decade if Black people were empowered to believe that everything in this country belongs to them, and they have the same rights to go out and accomplish whatever they want to? What would happen if we found our power?

I may have grown up in poverty for a portion of my life, but I matriculated through life without being handed a felony (although I've had a few close calls), I have three degrees, I've been an elected official, and through the grace of God have I obtained a level of financial security. However, what about the young woman who is very passionate about her community, but works at Walmart, and her shift doesn't allow her the flexibility to campaign for six months, and then serve in office for another four years? What about the parent who wants to attend the protest, and speak up for his community, but is afraid that if he does so, he will be fired from his job? Or what about the person who has lived in the area their entire life, noticed instances of injustice, oppression, bigotry, and racism, but has chalked it all up to "that's just the way things are around here." Patience, encouragement, and speaking life into a group of people who have seen their heroes knocked down, and their own thoughts pushed to the side is the empowerment work that is necessary. It's not enough for us to have one or two leaders, or to just rely on White people. I think that notion is changing.

In this fight against White Supremacy, we are going to have to multiply our efforts. Power and privilege go hand in hand; we just have to find it.

One ironic part about it all is that some White people already think that Black people have more privilege than anyone else in the country anyway.

"In America you can't even talk about Whiteness," said Drew Domalick, who lives in Green Bay, Wisconsin, in an interview with CNN in 2016. "If you try to embrace being White, you are portrayed as being a racist. If we had a White History Month, that would be viewed as a racist holiday."

"If you apply for a job, they seem to give the Blacks the first crack at it," added 68-year-old Tim Hershman of Akron, Ohio, "and, basically, you know, if you want any help from the government, if you're White, you don't get it. If you're Black, you get it."

On the surface, it may seem easy to dismiss these kinds of comments as foolishness. How can a group of people who have consistently been at the top of the proverbial food chain complain about reverse racism now that other people are finally getting a small piece of the pie? These people do not only believe that *reverse racism* exists; they contend that on a daily basis, Black people have the benefit of what they call Black privilege.

Instead of simply writing them off, I've dared to try to understand the logic behind how they have come to these conclusions. I have seen people take the approach of having civil conversations with racists and White supremacists and trying to understand their point of view while getting them to see the error of their ways. Sometimes it works, sometimes it doesn't. I have seen other people take the approach of yelling at them instead. Sometimes it works, sometimes it doesn't. It is not my job to tell you how to have conversations with White supremacists, racists, or people who can be classified no other way than as bigots. However, I do think that if we are going to attempt to defeat White Supremacy, we have to understand the nuances of how it came to be, and how it looks for the everyday White person who believes that either they are being treated unfairly, or believes that they aren't doing anything wrong.

Yes, we get it: the American nation was predicated on the premise that White people were inherently better than everyone else. It's well documented and understood how the system was started. However, I would like to explore the notion that the idea of "reverse racism" and even the thought of Black privilege is not a new phenomenon.

Since earning a spot on the Charlottesville City Council and being vocal about the need for change, I have become accustomed to receiving threats. My family has routinely received vile and disrespectful mail at our home, we have received calls during the middle of the night, and we have had bomb threats at my daughters' elementary school. I would be lying if I said that this is what I signed up for, but over time, I also understood that this was part of what comes with pushing for change. While on the city council, I had become accustomed to reading things like:

> "Keep up your bullshit and you will end up like Emmett Till."

> "Black lives matter only if they are picking cotton. Otherwise, hang their nigger asses!"

> "You are one stupid nigger with a death wish."

> "If you think the Whites of Charlottesville (or anywhere else for that matter) are going to vote themselves out of this colossal mess you're delusional. Things will only change when it's completely unsafe to go anywhere in public if you're White. Then White men will grow a set of balls again and end this stupidity. This nigger is TELLING everyone that he's a Black racist that puts Black interests first and all

Whites care about is college football (chock full of other Black racists) is starting this month."

The fact is I had learned to ignore the idiots, trolls, and social media commentators. I rarely if ever engaged in debates online, and for the most part, knew that there was no need to go back and forth with them. However, what about dealing with the people in real life who I had to encounter at the grocery store, at local restaurants with my family, the people who came to city council meetings, the people who came to my speeches who wanted to disrupt them, or undoubtedly the people in the community who often just stared at me but the others who had the courage to speak to me about how they felt that reverse racism and Black privilege was running rampant? What I learned over time was that in order to push to make a change in the world, the will power had to be developed to be patient with people and inpatient with progress. This reoccurring theme had become the mantra for my life.

To defeat White Supremacy, we have to operate in truth. However, truth is relative and often shaped through the lens of the individual. I want to be clear: I am not saying that we have to empathize, sympathize, or make excuses for White supremacists, people who are racists, or people who so afraid of change that they are willing to uphold hurtful and harmful practices and institutions. What I am saying though is that in order to defeat White Supremacy, we have to understand it, on some level. As this issue is one that is incredibly broad, expansive, and widespread, there are a multitude of people who can be described as White supremacists and/or racists. That in itself is a tough pill to swallow for a lot of people. The term "racist" is taboo in society; what normal person would want to be considered a racist? There is a large contingent of people in our society who really believe that the Civil War was about states' rights, not about slavery. There is a large contingent of people in our society who really believe that in the current world that we live in, White people are under attack. There is a large contingent of people who really believe in "reverse" racism. Are all of those people racist? Maybe, or maybe not, but I would ask each and every one of them *why* they believe those things?

Where did the terms "Black privilege" and "reverse racism" come from?

For that, we have to take a deeper dive into history. Roughly ten years after the Emancipation Proclamation, Congress passed a sweeping Civil Rights Act in 1875 that banned discrimination against former slaves in public places. However, the Supreme Court declared that act unconstitutional in 1883, a decision that sanctioned the rise of Jim Crow segregation and mob violence against Blacks that would last a century. So, take a step back and put that into prospective. In states in which slavery was legal, there were sets of laws known as "Slave Codes," which outlined the rights of slaves and the acceptable treatment and rules regarding them.

Some of the codes include:

- One could not do business with a slave without the prior consent of the owner.

- Slaves could be awarded as prizes in raffles, wagered in gambling, offered as security for loans, and transferred as gifts from one person to another.

- A slave was not permitted to keep a gun.

- If caught carrying a gun, the slave received 39 lashes and forfeited the gun.

- Blacks were held incompetent as witnesses in legal cases involving Whites.

- The education of slaves was prohibited.

- Anyone operating a school or teaching reading and writing to any African American in Missouri could be punished by a fine of not less than $500 and up to six months in jail.

- Slaves could not assemble without a White person present.

- Marriages between slaves were not considered legally binding. Therefore, owners were free to split up families.

- Any slave found guilty of arson, rape of a White woman, or conspiracy to rebel was put to death. However, since the slave woman was chattel, a White man who raped her was guilty only of a trespass on her master's property.

In the high court's 1883 decision, Justice Joseph Bradley wrote in the majority opinion that there must come a time when Blacks cease "to be the special favorite of the laws." So, think about that, a group of people who had just undergone some of the most inhumane treatment on the planet were told by the Chief Justice in the highest court in the United States of America that they needed to stop looking for special treatment from the law.

Presumably, Justice Bradley shared the sentiment of a lot of people (White people): Now that Blacks were free, they wanted all of these special provisions, and were trying to take over. Blacks should pull themselves up by the bootstraps and make their own way – but their way should make sure they stay in their place. Over the years, that sentiment bubbled to the surface at various times as debates over "reverse racism" and affirmative action erupted. However, if there is one thing that has become consistent over time, getting White people to admit that they have privilege, or that they benefit from a society built for them to succeed, or that they may be a just a tad bit racist – that's more challenging than getting President Trump to admit that climate change is real as the entire planet continues to get hotter and hotter.

Again, this isn't a new phenomenon. When segregationist Alabama Gov. George Wallace was asked by an interviewer in 1968 (CNN's Face the Nation) if he considered himself to be a racist, he said, "No sir, I don't regard myself as a racist, and I think the biggest racists in the world are those who call other folks racist. I think the biggest bigots in the world are those who call other folks bigots."

This is the same George Wallace who said in the 1963 Alabama Gubernatorial inauguration address, "Today I have stood, where once Jefferson Davis stood, and took an oath to my people. It is very appropriate then that from this Cradle of the Confederacy, this very Heart of the Great Anglo-Saxon Southland, that today we sound the drum for freedom as have our generations of forebears before us done, time and time again through history. Let us rise to the call of freedom-loving blood that is in us and send our answer to the tyranny that clanks its chains upon the South. In the name of the greatest people that have ever trod this earth, I draw the line in the dust and toss the gauntlet before the feet of tyranny . . . and I say . . . . segregation today . . . segregation tomorrow . . . segregation forever."

One of the best explanations of White privilege that I have read came from Brando Starkey of ESPN's *The Undefeated*. "Many White people rebut the notion that White privilege augments their lives," Starkey writes.

"That's because they consume the world in a specific manner, through what sociologist Joe Feagin calls the 'White racial frame.' Think of a frame as the process by which people take in new information, sift through the data, sort the important from the unimportant and decide how to feel about it all.

"Feagin argues that American culture has taught Whites to believe they represent the intellectual and cultural vanguard, to conclude that racial inequalities cannot be traced to their past or present behavior and to view their dominant status – their privilege – as natural and yet invisible.

"An example of how White people view their privilege as natural and invisible appears in Arlie Russell Hochschild's book Strangers in Their Own Land. She interviews working class and middle-class White people in Louisiana and learns they're disenchanted with their government and no longer recognize their country. They feel as if Black folk, other minorities, immigrants and refugees have cut ahead of them in line, meaning the government caters to others

before them. The line-cutting angers them, although they never question why they should occupy the first position. That implicit assumption – I should be tended to before all others – encapsulates how they view White privilege as natural and invisible.

"The White folk who most view the world through the White racial frame will interpret events to defend racial injustice and a Whites-on-top racial hierarchy. The wealth of evidence demonstrating police officers often brutalize Black people, for instance, establishes that Black people deserve the blame. The White racial frame deludes White folk into believing the system is operating as it should when it advantages them and disadvantages people of color.

I remember being downtown in Charlottesville staring at White supremacists with guns, swords, and all kinds of other weapons during the August 12 attack in 2017. I remember the painful shock as we watched a car drive into a group of peaceful protestors. I also distinctly remember President Trump coming on national television and saying that there were "evil people on both sides." In 2018, as the anniversary of the violent 2017 protests in Charlottesville arrived, Trump tweeted a condemnation of "all types" of racism. This was an obvious reference to the sort of reverse racism embedded in his and George Wallace's rhetoric: purported racism against White people.

The Washington Post in July 2019 published a report about Trump, his supporters, and their thoughts on "reverse racism" and how it was affecting their lives The Washington Post, *Trump embraces the 'reverse racism' feared by his supporters in a new 'squad' attack*), noting that a quarter of White people say they're very concerned about it. Research from the Pew Research Center released in March 2019 shows that White Republicans and Republican-leaning independents see Whites, Blacks and Hispanics as about equally the target of discrimination. (Philip Bump/The Washington Post)

Views among whites of extent of discrimination

Pew Research Center, March 2019

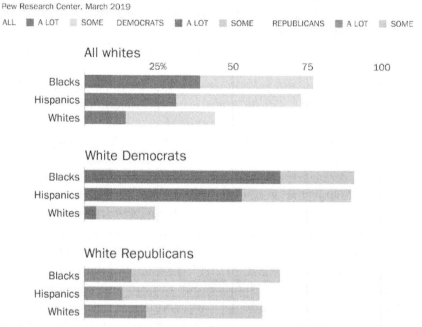

About a tenth of respondents told Pew that Whites face more discrimination than Blacks; 80 percent of that group identified as Republican or Republican leaning.

To conceptualize the data, I searched far and wide while speaking to White people from across the country so that I could understand how so many White people really believed what the data suggested. The best synopsis of it all came from James Blake in his 2016 CNN article *Black Privilege*.

> *"Where does this belief come from? The numbers don't appear to support it. Numerous studies and surveys show that Blacks lag behind Whites and other racial groups in many socioeconomic categories.*

> *"The wealth of White households is 13 times the median wealth of Black households. Black children represent 18% of the nation's preschool enrollment but make up nearly half of all children with multiple suspensions. Job applicants with*

White-sounding names are 50% more likely to get called back for an interview than similarly qualified applicants with Black-sounding names. And prison sentences for Black men are nearly 20% longer than those of White men convicted for similar crimes."

Some say you don't even need numbers to dismiss Black privilege. Use your eyes. If being Black is such an asset, why do many Whites consistently move out of communities – neighborhoods, churches, schools – when too many Blacks move in? It's a phenomenon that sociologists have long documented and that some call "racial tipping."

Those who argue for the existence of Black privilege, however, don't deny these grim numbers. They just don't blame racism for those racial disparities.

David Horowitz, author of the book, "Black Skin Privilege and the American Dream," says Blacks are still more privileged, though they lag behind other racial groups in varying categories. It's not White privilege that's preventing them from doing better, he says; it's their behavior, such as their inability to build more intact families.

"The fact that White people are better off is not a privilege; it's earned," says Horowitz, founder of the David Horowitz Freedom Center, a think tank in Los Angeles created to combat "the efforts of the radical left and its Islamist allies to destroy American values."

...Black privilege is so pervasive that it's hard to miss, he says. College professors practicing "affirmative grading" hold Black students to lower standards than others. Corporations offer programs and internships to Black workers but not to Whites.

Black privilege even extends to the White House, he says. Barack Obama was an inexperienced presidential candidate who was elected because Americans wanted to experience a post-racial sugar high, he says. "He wouldn't be elected dogcatcher if he wasn't Black," Horowitz says of Obama.

Some who invoke "Black privilege" also make another argument: Who says all unearned advantages are wrong?

In fact, some are unavoidable, says Benjamin Shapiro, a political commentator and author of an essay titled "Why White People Seek Black Privilege."

"Birth to a two-parent family is an unearned advantage. Birth into wealth is an unearned advantage. Being born smart or tall or athletic is an unearned advantage," Shapiro says. "But being born White in a rural backwater in West Virginia is not an advantage over being born the son of Colin Powell."

Blackness, though, has become a "tremendous asset" in contemporary America, he writes in his column. Despite the "horrific and evil history of racism against Black people," being Black today gives its recipients privileges ranging from landing coveted college scholarships to becoming activists who can build careers on racial grievances, he says.

More than half of Whites — 55 percent — surveyed say that, generally speaking, they believe there is discrimination against White people in America today. We heard it on the campaign trail at Trump rally after Trump rally. Donald Trump catered to White grievance during the 2016 presidential campaign and has done so as president as well.

Notable, however, is that while a majority of Whites in the poll say discrimination against them exists, a much smaller percentage say that they have actually experienced it. It is also important to note that 84 percent of Whites believe discrimination exists against racial and ethnic minorities in America today."

That argument is why Deborah Foster wrote an essay titled "A Guide to White Privilege for White People Who Think They've Never Had Any" which was published in HuffPost (formerly Huffington Post).

Foster says she grew up in an impoverished White family in Iowa where her parents were so poor, she was placed in foster care as a child because they couldn't afford to feed her.

Still, Foster says she experienced White privilege. She says she only knew that because she happened to live around poor Black people. She still had advantages that they did not, she says.

Her Black friends would get accused of stealing from stores; she wouldn't, even though she was with them. They would be suspended for missing too many classes or being late; she was placed in a gifted program, even though she also had attendance problems. They were called lazy Blacks behind their backs if they missed work at a fast-food restaurant; her behavior was never seen as a reflection on her race.

"We swim in White Supremacy, which makes it harder to point out unless you start looking for it," she says."

After speaking to a lot of people who didn't necessarily look like me, and reading extensively about the topic, I began to think about those conversations, and honestly there was a realization that I was coming to. The sooner I stopped calling every person who disagreed with me a racist, the sooner I would be able to change minds. However, in order to change minds, I had to be willing to do what some others didn't want to do: vigorously fight White Supremacy on the front lines through policy and protest, but still leave room in my heart to have one-on-one conversations with racists and White supremacists about the topic of race.

I came to realize that different people required different approaches. Some people can come to understand their racism through data. Some can understand systemic oppression through story. Some people can understand the error of their ways through the pain of protest. What was painfully obvious is that there is no single way to combat this issue: to fight White Supremacy, we have to be the human form of a Swiss Army knife. Tiring, for sure. Necessary, nonetheless.

Loving Blackness, lifting up Blackness, and asserting Black Power can be frightening for a lot of White folks who just don't understand, *who refuse to understand.* It can be frightening to a lot of Black people too. So do we allow our fears to consume us? Or do we push through and find the will to be the change that we are looking for? The choice is only one that we make on our own time.

5. HOW CAN WE WIN?

When Black women talk, it is normally a good idea for all of us to listen. The following words are from my sister Kimberly Latrice Jones. During the summer of 2020, our country saw a reaction in the streets unlike anything that we have seen before. When it comes to the "right" way for Black people to protest, or express themselves, or build their own community, or become self-sufficient, or well... you get the point, there are many opinions. I feel like this sister summed it perfectly. White people, remove your privilege and listen up. Black people, take a deep breath, find your power. Everyone, listen, learn, and then act.

"I have been seeing a lot of things, people making commentary – interestingly enough, the ones that I have seen making the commentary, are wealthy Black people, making commentary that we should not be rioting, we should not be looting, we should not be tearing up our own community. Then on the other side, there has been commentary that we should be hitting them in the pocket. We should be focusing on the blackout days where we don't spend money. I feel like we should do both. I feel like we should support both, and I will tell you why I support both. I support both, because when you have civil unrest like this you have three types of people in the streets. There are the protestors, there are the rioters, and there are the looters.

The protestors are there because they actually care about what is happening in the community, they want to raise their voices, and they are there strictly to protest. You have the rioters who are angry, who are anarchists, who really just want to fuck shit up, and that is what they are going to do, regardless. And then you have the looters, the looters are almost exclusively there to do just that, to loot. People are like "Well what did you get? What did you gain from looting?" I think that as long as we are focusing on the *what*, we are not focusing on the *why*, and that is my issue with that. As long as we are focusing on what they are doing, we are not focusing on why they are doing it. Some people are like "Well those aren't people who are legitimately angry about what's happening. Those are people who just want to get stuff." Ok, so let's go with that, let's say that it is exactly what is. Now let's ask ourselves, "Why in this country, in 2020, the financial gap between poor Blacks and the rest of the world is at such a distance that people feel like their only hope and only opportunity to get some of the things that we flaunt and flash in front of them all of the time is to walk through a broken glass window and get it? Why do they feel that they are so hopeless that getting that necklace, getting that TV, getting that chain, getting that bed, getting that phone, or whatever it is that they are going to get, that in that moment when the riot happened and if the riots present an opportunity of looting that is their only opportunity to get it. We need to be questioning *that* why. *Why* are people that poor? *Why* are people that broke? *Why* are people that food insecure, that clothing insecure? *Why* do people feel that their only shot, that they are shooting their shot by walking through a broken glass window to get what they need. And then people want to talk about "Well there are plenty of people who pulled themselves up by their own bootstraps, and got it on their own, why can't they do that?"

Let me explain something to you about economics in America. I am so glad that as a young child I got an opportunity to spend time at P.U.S.H. where they taught me this. We must never forget that economics was the reason that Black people were bought to this country. We came to do the agriculture work in the South, and the textile work in the North. Do you understand that? That is what we came to do. We came to do the agriculture work in the South, and the textile work in the North. Now if I right now decided that I wanted to play monopoly with you, and for 400 rounds of playing Monopoly I didn't allow you to have any money, I didn't allow you to have anything on the board, I didn't allow for you to have anything. Then we played another 50 rounds of monopoly, and everything that you gained and you earned while you playing during those rounds of Monopoly was taken from you. That was Tulsa, that was Rosewood. Those are places that we built Black economic wealth, where we were self-sufficient, where we owned our stores, we owned our property, and they burned them to the ground. So that's 450 years. So for 400 rounds of Monopoly, you don't get to play at all. Not only do you not get to play, you have to play on the behalf of the person that you are playing against. You have to play, and make money, and earn wealth for them, and then you have to turn it over to them. So then for 50 years you finally get a little bit and you are allowed to play, and every time that they don't like the way that you're playing, or that you're catching up, or that you are doing something to be self-sufficient, they burn your game, they burn your cards, they burn your Monopoly money. Then finally, at the release and the onset of that, they allow you to play, and they say, "Ok, now you catch up." Now at this point the only way that you are going to catch up in the game is if the other person shares the wealth, correct? But what if every time they shared the wealth, there is psychological warfare going against you calling you an "equal opportunity hire"?

So if I played 400 rounds of Monopoly with you, and I have to play and give you every dime that I made, and then for 50 years, every time that I played, if you didn't like what I did and got to burn it, like they did in Tulsa or like they did in Rosewood, how can you win? *How* can you win? You *can't* win. The game is fixed. So when they say "Why do you burn down the community? Why do you burn down your own neighborhood?" It's *not* ours. We don't own anything! We don't own ANYTHING!

Trevor Noah said it so beautifully last night. There is a social contract that we all have. If you steal or I steal, the person who is the authority comes in, and they fix the situation. But the person who is supposed to fix the situation is KILLING US! So the social contract is broken! And if the social contract is broken, why the fuck do I give a shit about burning a fucking College Football Hall of Fame or about burning a fucking Target? You broke the contract when you killed us in the streets, and didn't give a fuck! You broke the contract when for over 400 years we played your game and built your wealth! You broke the contract when we built our wealth again, on our own, by our bootstraps in Tulsa, and you dropped bombs on us. When we built it in Rosewood, and you came in and slaughtered us! YOU broke the contract, so fuck your Target, Fuck your Hall of Fame. As far as I'm concerned, they can burn this bitch to the ground, and it still would not be enough. And they are lucky that what Black people are looking for is equality, and not revenge.

- Kimberly Latrice Jones

6. NO RECONCILIATION OR HEALING WITHOUT REPARATIONS – POLICY AND PROGRESSION IN THE 21ST CENTURY

The mere thought of reparations in America usually makes people think of one of three things. For a lot of White people, the thought is "Why do I have to pay for something that I personally did not do? I've never owned slaves. Why do my taxes have to pay for this?" Others follow a model that believes that something needs to be done to help balance out the generational wealth that has been ripped away due to our country's past. There are other people who believe that reparations in some form are needed, that it's the least the country can do to compensate for centuries of harm. Still others believe that the past is the past, and all that we can do is move forward with trying to improve the present and the future.

It's clear that the topic of reparations is one that cannot be resolved in a vacuum, and will not be resolved in a day, month, year, or in some cases, a decade. However, I am convinced that something has to be done.

One of the biggest lessons I learned while I was in elected office was just how policy shapes the day-to-day lives of people. In order to level the playing field in any capacity, specifically for Black people, there has to be strategic and targeted measures to ensure that the wrongs of yesteryear are corrected.

For many, the need for dialogue to help improve race relations is paramount. While I too desire more dialogue and understand why some prefer comfortable conversation that is non-confrontational, I believe that it is not, by itself, a recipe for success. In order to create change and bring forth equity in our society as a whole, there will have to be some form of reckoning with the wrongs that our nation has done to people of African descent. Reparations.

Before actual reparations can come to fruition, the actual meaning behind the "40 acres and a mule" idea must be explained. Here is an excerpt from esteemed scholar and Harvard University professor Dr. Henry Louis Gates, Jr. about the origin of the model.

> *"We've all heard the story of the "40 acres and a mule" promise to former slaves. It's a staple of black history lessons, and it's the name of Spike Lee's film company. The promise was the first systematic attempt to provide a form of reparations to newly freed slaves, and it was astonishingly radical for its time, proto-socialist in its implications. In fact, such a policy would be radical in any country today: the federal government's massive confiscation of private property — some 400,000 acres — formerly owned by Confederate land owners, and its methodical redistribution to former black slaves. What most of us haven't heard is that the idea really was generated by black leaders themselves.*

> **What Exactly Was Promised?**

> *We have been taught in school that the source of the policy of "40 acres and a mule" was Union General William T. Sherman's Special Field Order No. 15, issued on Jan. 16,*

78

1865. (That account is half-right: Sherman prescribed the 40 acres in that Order, but not the mule. The mule would come later.) But what many accounts leave out is that this idea for massive land redistribution actually was the result of a discussion that Sherman and Secretary of War Edwin M. Stanton held four days before Sherman issued the Order, with 20 leaders of the black community in Savannah, Ga., where Sherman was headquartered following his famous March to the Sea. The meeting was unprecedented in American history.

What Became of the Land That Was Promised?

The response to the Order was immediate. When the transcript of the meeting was reprinted in the black publication Christian Recorder, an editorial note intoned that "From this it will be seen that the colored people down South are not so dumb as many suppose them to be," reflecting North-South, slave-free black class tensions that continued well into the modern civil rights movement. The effect throughout the South was electric: As Eric Foner explains, "the freedmen hastened to take advantage of the Order." Baptist minister Ulysses L. Houston, one of the group that had met with Sherman, led 1,000 blacks to Skidaway Island, Ga., where they established a self-governing community with Houston as the "black governor." And by June, "40,000 freedmen had been settled on 400,000 acres of 'Sherman Land.'" By the way, Sherman later ordered that the army could lend the new settlers mules; hence the phrase, "40 acres and a mule."

And what happened to this astonishingly visionary program, which would have fundamentally altered the course of American race relations? Andrew Johnson, Lincoln's successor and a sympathizer with the South, overturned the Order in the fall of 1865, and, as Barton Myers sadly concludes, "returned the land along the South Carolina,

Georgia and Florida coasts to the planters who had originally owned it" — to the very people who had declared war on the United States of America.

The notion that the descendants of enslaved Africans in America are entitled to 40 acres and a mule is based on documented evidence. However, just as has been the norm for most things pertaining to Black folk in this nation, the promise was snatched away by policy change. Our country is a nation built on practices, policies, laws, and White Supremacy. Combatting such change requires a lot of individual work, but even more collective work by policy makers. There can be no healing or moments of racial harmony without a reallocation of resources. Anything other than intentional reallocation of resources by policy makers on a local, state, and federal level is nothing more than lip service.

In the eyes of some, this may seem harsh. In the eyes of others, it may seem like an impossible task. In the eyes of those who are looking to combat and defeat White Supremacy, resource reallocation is both necessary and doable. One way for municipalities on a local level to address the wrongs of the past is to analyze the city budget and be strategic in how they allocate resources to marginalized and underserved communities. As an elected official in Charlottesville, VA, two of my proudest moments were the City Council's adoption of the "Equity Package" and the "Business Equity Fund." Both policy changes resulted in multimillion-dollar budget allocations to marginalized communities and had a direct and immediate impact on African American people. While these initiatives may have been my idea, I could not have gotten them into policy without my colleagues and members of the public who got on board and lobbied for them. Racism, White Supremacy, and the ills of our country are not going to be cured by one or two people. These issues are not going to be solved overnight or in silos. The fact of the matter remains that very few Black people control the resources in our nation; therefore, by default we have to build power among ourselves and have partners who are willing to help us in this fight. That fight will require more than talking, but targeted action.

Message to Black and White people: Equity is Transactional

I am a firm believer that we have the ability to rid our country of racism within the next 100 years. Oftentimes when I say this during my speeches, regardless of the audience, people look at me with disbelief. The fact that the institution as we know as America was built on racism and White Supremacy is something that will always be true. However, just because the past was that way does not mean that the future has to repeat the past. In my opinion, the number one way that both Black people and White people work together to eradicate racism is through changing policy: educational policy, criminal justice policy, economic policy, human rights policy, environmental policy, and so forth are the fundamental tools to leveling the proverbial playing field. It is often said within Black social circles when the topic of race arises, specifically when discussing symbolic measures like the removal of Confederate statues, "Moving them statues ain't going to change what's in their (White people) hearts." Yes, that is true, but for some people, to be honest, I don't really care what's in their hearts. I think we worry too much about how someone feels about us as individuals. In my opinion, questions about whether or not someone does or doesn't like me based on the color of my skin are fruitless. What matters most is how they treat me. If they fake it, fine. As long as they are faking their respect for me that leads to progressive change, cool. The moment that they choose to show, do, or act otherwise, there have to be policies in place to hold them accountable. Some people reading will say that even with policies in place, the people who are enforcing the policies have to be fair, and repeatedly, we have seen that to not be true. This is where the challenging work for both Black people and White people must be focused.

Step 1: Develop   and implement equitable policies and a

redistribution of resources.

Step 2: Create and sustain a system for equity to maintain, preserve, and protect the policies.

Many people who watched the White supremacists march up and down the streets of Charlottesville believe that they were there to protest the removal of the statue of Robert E. Lee. As noted in my book, **Monumental: It Was Never about a Statue**, this is inaccurate. The Unite the Right Rally was never about the statue. It was about the changing of a system in which people who were traditionally in positions of power were being moved and equitable practices being followed through. It was about the power of multiple races, ethnicities, faiths, and age demographics fighting back against White supremacist values. The single greatest example of unity took place on both a symbolic and substantive scale in our city – a true model for the country. The symbolic piece was the call for the removal of the statue of Robert E. Lee and all of the Black and White people who stood together in unity, who were persistent and consistent in the call for the removal, and who stood vigilantly against the Ku Klux Klan and tiki torch mob each time they came to our city. The substantive piece of this puzzle was potentially the greatest piece of political maneuvering and resource reallocation in our city's modern history: The Equity Package. The Equity Package (which I wrote, my White colleague on City Council Kristin Szakos edited, and another White colleague, Bob Fenwick, supported) coupled with the vote to remove the statues, was a prime example of Black and White elected officials standing together to achieve the goal of moving the community forward. Included in the Equity Package was nearly $4 million in resources to underserved communities, with the largest impact being felt within the local African American population within the city. The package included the following:

Education:

Charlottesville Scholarship Program:

- In honor of former mayors Rev. Dr. Alvin Edwards, Charles Barbour, Vice-Mayor Dr. Holly Edwards, and others who have served on this same city council, City Council will establish a **$5,000-a-year** scholarship through the Charlottesville Scholarship Program in their name for Charlottesville City Schools graduates to attend an Historically Black College or University (HBCU) of their choice.

GED Training and Course Assistance:

- City Council will allocate up to **$20,000** to work with the Charlottesville Housing Authority and the Adult Learning Program, to provide free GED training and cover the cost of the GED exams for residents of our Public Housing sites and work to seek assistance for at least 50% of the tuition to PVCC for these GED completers.

Course Curriculum in Local Schools

- City Council will offer a grant of **$15,000** for the creation of an Ethnic Studies course to be taught in our local schools, focusing on the history of people of color in the City of Charlottesville, in conjunction with the Charlottesville City Schools. This course will comply with all Standards of Learning (SoL) guidelines and requirements, and will expose local students to the history, the difficulties, accomplishments, and impact of people of color in and around the City of Charlottesville.

Coordinator for Black Youth Achievement:

- As initially proposed by the Charlottesville Youth Council, this new position (est. cost **$100,000** including salary, benefits and program budget) will focus on a community-wide effort to close gaps in opportunity and achievement in education and employment, coordinate and inform the work of non-profit and other community partners, and work with young African-American residents of

Charlottesville to develop leadership skills, academic excellence and workforce readiness. This position may be housed in the Office of Human Services, Human Rights or the City Manager.

Housing

- Charlottesville City Council will prioritize the allocation of **$2.5 million** dollars over the next five years into the City's Capital Improvement Plan for redevelopment of our local Public Housing.
- City Council and lead staff will convene a Town Hall meeting to explain in detail the partnership between City Council, CRHA, and PHAR for the new CACF grant. The program will include a clear explanation to the public of:
  - o the process of the Affordable Housing Fund,
  - o where the city currently stands in regards to affordable housing, and
  - o the current plan for increasing more affordable housing.
- City Council tasks staff with conducting a series of meetings and public education workshops to inform neighbors and concerned organizations in the SIA area and involve them in its implementation, including explanations of form-based code and initiatives in the SIA, and using input from those participants to help ensure that development does not displace low-wealth communities in the SIA while increasing the stock of affordable and moderately priced housing.

Workforce Training and Employment

- Charlottesville City Council will prioritize workforce training for residents who live in the SIA to assist with upward mobility.
- The City will continue to push the GO Initiative in low-wealth communities throughout the City.

- The Black Youth Achievement director will help to staff Circle of Brotherhood and other targeted employment and training initiatives for young people of color

Jefferson School African American Heritage Center

- Charlottesville City Council will provide a one-time grant of **$950,000** to the Jefferson School African American Heritage Center to provide assistance for this staple of the Charlottesville Community, and to ensure the successful refinancing of the building that will ensure its long-term viability.

Dialogue on Race

- Dr. Holly Edwards and several other community leaders were the visionaries and driving forces behind the local Dialogue on Race in 2010. City Council will allocate **$10,000** to the Human Rights Commission and task this group with prioritizing a second round of the Dialogue on Race to the Charlottesville Community.

Slave Auction Block

- In accordance with the Blue-Ribbon Commission Report, Charlottesville City Council will allocate **$50,000** for a design competition and reinterpretation of the current slave auction block.

Tonsler Park

- In an effort to create equity throughout the city. It has been stated that as short as two years ago, in the City's Capital Improvement Plan, we the City Council, task staff to put the necessary monies, **$250,000** back into the CIP for the construction of a Field House at Tonsler Park.

When some people think of reparations, they believe it comes in the form of what will be the equivalent of 40 acres and a mule which would be a massive payout or payment to every person who identifies or is identified as Black by today's standards. Admittedly, I completely understand, and honestly, wish this would come to fruition, we have to be very honest with ourselves about the fact that it will never come in that form. While the debate can continue nationally about how to allocate and distribute reparations, legislatures on both the state and local level can use policy and budgets to make amends in the immediate. This requires elected officials to be willing to think outside of the box, exude some of their political will, and most importantly, work together. In part, when we talk about reparations, society has proven for generations that Black people with the same profiles as Whites have been denied loans from Banks. In the simplest form, even our financial institutions have policies rooted and based in White Supremacy, denying Black people access to capital, which in turn is one of the reasons why there is such a strong wealth gap between Blacks and Whites in America. While on a day to day level, the systems that have been put in place are so deeply rooted, that it feels as is nothing can be done. However, policies can be changed. Resources can be reallocated. Change can be made.

In 2018, I put together a local policy known as the Business Equity Fund to address the needs of "Socially Disadvantaged Persons" a federal designation, to help level the playing field in the business community. In essence, the Business Equity Fund, or BEF, provides up to $25,000 to business owners to either start their business or scale up their business. I convinced my colleagues on city council to allocate $109,000 in funding in partnership with a local non-profit to administer the program, and within six months, we saw nearly ten Black owned businesses take apply for and receive funding, start or scale up their business, hire new people from the community, and subsequently move our community in a different direction. While it is not us giving money directly in the hands of those who have had to undergo the most brutal and worst parts of our history, it does provide a tangible path to righting a wrong.

For their courage to change policy, to be brave enough to go against the proverbial grain of White Supremacy, for the power to choose what is right over what has historically been wrong, my colleagues faced threats, one lost reelection, and in the eyes of some they were traitors. Their sacrifice of self for the greater good of policy is what was needed, and an example for people across the country. When we fight together for what is right, and do so willingly and unapologetically, our communities, our cities, our nation becomes a better place. Our country doesn't need a White savior or a Black savior. Our country just needs people to stand up for what is right, moral and just. Again, we do this by changing policy.

Message to White People:

The need for resource allocation is vital to the defeating of White Supremacy, and White people are going to have to play a strong role in this effort. Specifically, for elected officials in this space, the need for your voice in correcting the wrongs of past generations, the wrongs of elected bodies before you, and in some cases, the wrongs of your own administration will require a level of courage that many are unaccustomed to. I am here to warn you, this will be tough. People who you believe are your friends will call you names. People who you have known your entire lives will say things about you that you didn't they were capable of. People who you have served with will look at you sideways for your commitment to equity. Some of the people who voted for you will tell you that they will no longer support your campaign financially, and people have been staunch supporters of yours will fall by the wayside. These actions will hurt your feelings. These actions will make you question your commitment to equity and wonder if it's worth it. The very people who you are looking to support may question your motives and ask you repeatedly why are you now pushing towards equity. It will be incredibly challenging. However, with all of that said, it will be beyond worth it. The reward that you are looking for will not come from people. The gratification that you are seeking will not come from voters. The joy will come from knowing that you played a role in your particular city, state, or municipality in correcting a wrong. The joy will come from creating a legacy of doing what is right to help defeat White Supremacy. For that, I want to say I encourage you to push through all negativity. Furthermore, I want to thank you for your courage.

Message to Black people:

My brothers and sisters, we are all aware that the current system is not designed for us to win. While this is indeed a fact, it does not mean that we can afford to sit on the proverbial sidelines and be paralyzed by the inequities around us. We all are going to have to find out what our role is in the movement for equity. Specifically, for the elected officials, each and every single one of us will need to call on the spirit of the ancestors and push for bold policies that will reallocate resources to our people. Yes, it will make people call you names on social media, and potentially you will lose some votes, however it will be well worth it. Yes, you will need to be strategic and, in some cases, do some political maneuvering to ensure that you have the votes needed, but it can be done. Over 31 cities across the country have adopted some variation of the "Equity Package" and at the time of this writing, nearly 50 more were working on such documents.

7. THE EQUALIZERS DON'T MAKE US EQUAL

White Supremacy comes in several different forms, but to make things easy, I like to view it in one of two pots: the covert and the overt. I will never forget the day when I first saw the sign being held by what I thought was a young man, close to my age, that read "Wes Bellamy, Go Be a Nigger Somewhere else." The boldness of it all shook me to my core. It raised an emotion within me that wanted to fight, that wanted to yell, that wanted to retaliate in a way that would undoubtedly send me to jail, but at least I would get my money's worth. You see, overt White Supremacy wants to do just that. It wants to bring forth an emotion within us all that makes us feel so angry that we become irrational. More often than not, historically, the perpetuators of overt White Supremacy have been White people who are reluctant to change – White people who believe that they are superior to every other race on the planet. White people who are committed to testing the limits of social norms and are ok with spewing their racial or religious animus at whomever they deem fit for it. Again, it wants you to react. It is often hilarious to see their faces when you don't take the bait.

Covert racism is much more methodical. It involves systems, it involves people, it involves the willing, the conscious, and in many instances, works so well that a lot of people partake in it daily, and don't even know it. A lot of people, especially White people, live

89

with false pretenses when it comes to race. It's not every White person's fault, per se. As in you as an individual, that these systems have been created. Let's take Pittsburgh for example. You have The Hill District, which is one of the more predominant African American neighborhoods in the city. In my opinion, Pittsburgh as a city, is a microcosm of the United States of America, especially with how we truly address matters revolving around race and the root cause of issues.

Pittsburgh has large pockets of Black people living mostly in one or two areas (pre-gentrification) due to a variety of reasons. Red-lining kept Black people separate from the rest of the city, banks refused to give Black people loans for a home in a different neighborhood, banks refused to give Black people loans to start their businesses, a large portion of the community received a poor education, and over policing was so common that people thought it was normal to be harassed. Not that we are trying to take advantage of the situation or make excuses, but we are forced to play the hand that we are dealt. That is coupled with the fact that as a race of people, for hundreds of years it was outlawed for us to know how to read, and/or provided with less than, and expected to do more with. We are placed in food deserts, in which the only place in which you can get food is the convenience store, kids are eating Hot Cheetos and Doritos for breakfast, and subsequently these same students are being asked to perform at the same rate as their pupils who don't have to deal with any of these perils or students who have full course meals for breakfast, lunch, and dinner. And then we wonder why in those same neighborhoods where there are also no jobs, we wonder why people are harming each other? Then we ask ourselves, well how do we get the homicide rate down? We look at each other, have meetings, that lead to other meetings, and ask ourselves how can we stop the murders in these particular communities? We ignore the fact that this entire system has been created by people who sit in the same positions as you and I (elected office), and then those same individuals who are in my position look at folks who are harming each other, not because they innately hate each other, but because they see no way out. The only way that I see myself getting out of this position is if I harm you. By harming you, it allows me to assert my dominance in the proverbial food chain, and in some cases, this is the only way I find value in myself and/or how I can make money. And then we say well we need to figure out how we can partner with a community group, probably pay them 1/5 of what we received the grant to help the people in the community for, and figure out how to help "these people" empower themselves and solve these systemic issues. Again, it's not one individual's fault, but to me it is one of the most mind-boggling and frustrating aspects of the current landscape of creating change and convincing people to think outside of the box.

When we talk about discussions and forums, those aren't the real conversations that we are having. We don't spend enough time on the Block in the community asking *why* someone is so upset and would feel the need to make poor choices?

Response: Well I am upset because I don't have a job.

Well, why don't you have a job?

Response: Well when I was in the 9th grade, I wasn't the best reader and my teachers told me that I was headed for prison because I always got suspended in school. So, I dropped out of school.

Well, why did you drop out of school?

Response: Well also I needed to take care of my three little brothers and sisters at home, because my mom had to piece together three different incomes from three different temp jobs to put food on the table and keep the lights on.

Well, why is she working three jobs?

Response: Because she had a pretty bad experience at the local school. She didn't like it, and I guess it kind of just passed down to me. And the man that she chose to be with, my real dad, he left us.

Well, why did he leave?

Response: Basically because he felt that he couldn't handle it all. He had mental health issues. He was depressed in some ways,

The overarching point is that the issues are a lot deeper than just this blanket approach is going to help our communities. The White Supremacy in a lot of this allows us to say things like the people in these situations are lazy, or that they don't want more for themselves, or some other negative connotation that we associate with this specific demographic opposed to truly analyzing and addressing the systemic root causes which have led to issues of today. The elected officials will come up with a spicy new initiative, say let's partner with the police and the token community group, and the police department, host a press conference and then all is well. This is frustrating, because it often feels as if many of us today, even with the massive amount of intelligence that we possess and the constant stories of the same playbook being ineffective refuse to truly deal with the root of the matter. It was White Supremacy hundreds of years ago, and it is still White Supremacy causing a great deal of the aforementioned today. A blanket approach will not help us. The same strategies from decades ago that we have seen regurgitated today from 30 years ago are not the solution. We can't settle for minimum progress, a few people getting crumbs, and then subsequently we believe that we have won. The homicide rate going down two to three percentage points over a three-year span is not true progress. That does not allow for your District Attorneys, Attorney Generals, Police Departments, or elected officials to claim victory, because the two to three percentage point decrease more often than not still leaves us with a number that would be absolutely abhorrent, atrocious, and unacceptable in predominately White communities, cities, and municipalities. If the lack of crime and abundance of resources is a good formula for affluent predominantly White spaces, why are the same resources and converted efforts not made to Black communities and communities of color? In my opinion, this is the flawed method that cities, counties, municipalities, and several grassroots

92

organizations run into. It's not enough for us to have small wins, because we went from 30 shootings to 26 shootings in a year, doesn't mean that we won or that we have solved the issue. We still haven't dealt with the real issue. It's not that I am shooting you because I hate you. I am shooting you because I am hungry, I am emotionally undeveloped. I don't know how to cope or deal with my own issues and I don't understand why I am stuck in this neighborhood. I don't understand the nuances of navigating the job interview process or how to legitimately become an entrepreneur, so I am going to sell him heroine and sell her crack because this is literally the only way that I believe that I can make money to put food on the table to help my mother who is working three jobs put food on the table, keep the lights on, and get my little brothers and sisters the school clothes that they need or the $20 that it cost to go on the 2nd grade class trip because my little brother wants to go and I don't want him to be the only person in his class who doesn't get to make it. These are the real issues that are the byproducts of the systems set up by White Supremacy that require long hours to solve. They require stepping out of our comfort zones to address. These are the problems that the elders can't just pray away. These are the issues that you can't change overnight without actually showing up. To create this change, you can't tweet your way out of it, can't Snapchat your way out of it, and if you remain stagnant it will only get worse.

I ask this question all of the time. What are you willing to sacrifice to be the change that we all know we need? If it was easy, then everyone would have already done it.

Education – The Great Equalizer

Ever since I was a little kid, I was told that education was the great equalizer. My family members, my pastor, my coaches, the guys in the neighborhood, and everywhere else, people would consistently reiterate the importance of education. I was an avid reader growing up, after in the 7th grade, my childhood crush told me that she only liked guys who read. Two of my older cousins – who were more like older sisters—were also avid readers, and I loved to read the street novels that they consumed. Stories about Black history and books about the importance changed my life during my middle school and early high school years, and I began to see the benefits of my acumen for reading. My vocabulary was expansive, I saw the world differently from a lot of my friends, because I had read about the differences. This shaped my thirst for knowledge, and I truly believed that if I was educated, I would be able to level the playing field with my counterparts. This was a fallacy.

While I eventually went on to become a high school teacher for six years, a Dean of Students at an alternative high school, a college professor, college department chair, and was even appointed to the Virginia State Board of Education, I must admit something that a lot of people already know. The current education system is so flawed, that for a lot of Black people it feels as if it is rigged.

To date, there have been countless studies and information produced showing the inequities in the current education system in America. To be clear, the National Criminal Justice Reference Service defines "Racial disparity" as existing in the criminal justice system when "the proportion of a racial/ethnic group within the control of the system is greater than the proportion of such groups in the general population." Furthermore, illegitimate or unwarranted racial disparity results from differential treatment by the criminal justice system of similarly situated people based on race. In some instances, this may involve overt racial bias, and in others it may reflect the influence of factors that are only indirectly associated with race.

The United Negro College Fund, a philanthropic organization that works diligently to fund scholarships, provide internships, and advocates for students who attend Historically Black Colleges and Universities, recently published a report with a series of data points pointing out racial disparities in the education system.

STATISTIC #1:

African American students are less likely than White students to have access to college-ready courses. In fact, in 2011-12, only 57 percent of Black students have access to a full range of math and science courses necessary for college readiness, compared to 81 percent of Asian American students and 71 percent of White students.

STATISTIC #2:

Even when Black students do have access to honors or advanced placement courses, they are vastly underrepresented in these courses. Black and Latino students represent 38 percent of students in schools that offer AP courses, but only 29 percent of students enrolled in at least one AP course. Black and Latino students also have less access to gifted and talented education programs than White students.

STATISTIC #3:

Research has shown evidence of systematic bias in teacher expectations for African American students and non-Black teachers were found to have lower expectations of Black students than Black teachers.

STATISTIC #4:

Black students spend less time in the classroom due to discipline, which further hinders their access to a quality education. Black students are nearly two times as likely to be suspended without educational services as White students. Black students are also 3.8 times as likely to receive one or more out-of-school suspensions as White students. In addition, Black children represent 19 percent of the nation's pre-school population, yet 47 percent of those receiving more than one out-of-school suspension. In comparison, White students represent 41 percent of pre-school enrollment but only 28 percent of those receiving more than one out-of-school suspension. Even more troubling, Black students are 2.3 times as likely to receive a referral to law enforcement or be subject to a school-related arrest as White students.

STATISTIC #5:

Students of color are often concentrated in schools with fewer resources. Schools with 90 percent or more students of color spend $733 less per student per year than schools with 90 percent or more White students.

STATISTIC #6:

In 2015, the average reading score for White students on the National Assessment of Educational Progress (NAEP) 4th and 8th grade exam was 26 points higher than Black students. Similar gaps are apparent in math. The 12th grade assessment also show alarming disparities as well, with only seven percent of Black students performing at or above proficient on the math exam in 2015, compared to 32 percent White students.

There is a clear lack of Black representation in school personnel. According to a 2016 Department of Education report, in 2011-12, only 10 percent of public-school principals were Black, compared to 80 percent White. Eighty-two percent of public-school educators are White, compared to 18 percent teachers of color. In addition, Black male teachers only constitute two percent of the teaching workforce.

When we analyze data that show the clear disparities within the education system, they can seem somewhat overwhelming. However, I think the data and the disparities by race are the byproduct of something much deeper. The root cause of the issue is multifaceted, and my experiences led me to see several chinks in the armor, which are rooted in White Supremacy. The mind-boggling piece is that the covert racism that is prevalent is so masked that the average person, both Black and White, don't usually see. It requires one to think critically about the issues to even recognize the problem, and the issues themselves require a herculean effort to solve them.

If education is the great equalizer in society, and Black males are continuously lagging behind in nearly every academic category and surpassing all other demographics in every negative disciplinary category, why not just hire more Black men to be teachers to help quell the issue. Black males represent roughly 2% of the total teaching population in America, and my friends and I all can count on one hand the amount of Black male teachers we had throughout our K-12 career. Why is that? Is it because brothers don't want to teach? Do school systems not need us? Do little kids not need to see us? The answer is complex, and in 2017, I wrote my dissertation about the Perceptions of Black male educators in Central Virginia, and my findings were interesting to say the least. White Supremacy is so entrenched in the inertia of our everyday lives that many of us don't even see it in the systems that we all participate in. When it came to the research, I interviewed nearly 300 people via survey. Because I wanted to examine the perceptions of African American Male Educators in the K–12 school system in Central Virginia, this study focused solely on the opinions of this specific subgroup, with the exception of when they were being compared to their White Male counterparts in the K–12 school system. Implications and correlations can be made about how strongly the respondent felt about the need and/or value of Black educators based on the race of the respondent. The findings from this study were interesting to say the least. A variety of different variables were taken into account including race, age, teaching experience, educational background, and a host of other factors. While the themes appeared to demonstrate that Black male educators need to be recruited, that they are effective, and that they need to be compensated, morally supported, and placed in healthy school environments in order to be successful, I am perplexed as to why these issues have yet to be solved. I was intrigued by some of the findings for several reasons. While analyzing the responses based on the length of teaching experience, the view of how the educator perceived the effectiveness of the Black Male teacher varied.

Educators with less than ten years of experience were more likely to both strongly agree that Black male educators should be recruited and that they were effective. This is point is alarming considering the fact that across the region most principals, central office personnel, and those who determine advancement for Black Male educators have more than ten years of experience in the field. So, while it appears that Black Males are considered very effective by community stakeholders, if they are not seen as strongly effective by educators with more experience nor believed that they should be recruited in the same manner as community stakeholders. The community could very well want more Black Male educators in different places throughout the school system, and the decision makers, in comparison to their counterparts, could not view them in the same light as their White male counterparts. This could be one explanation as to why we see so few Black Males not only in our classrooms, but in different educational leadership positions throughout the school divisions throughout the region. Furthermore, if you look at most of the people who serve in the Central office of your local school divisions, the majority of them are White, and more often than not, White men. I'll allow you to draw your own conclusions from here.

I have been told that in addition to the education being the great equalizer, having money would allow access to a variety of things, and to a certain extent, also level the proverbial playing field. However, this too was a fallacy.

According to a recent article published by National Public Radio (NPR) *"Graduates of Historically Black Colleges May Be Paying More For Loans: Watchdog Group."*

It is common knowledge for many about historic prejudice practices as it pertains to lending practices by banks and financial institutions.

"Financial firms may be discriminating against people based

on where they went to college, a watchdog group says. In particular, the group found that a lender named Upstart appears to be charging higher interest rates on student loans to graduates of historically Black or predominantly Hispanic colleges.

A lot more people are getting loans these days from a new breed of lenders known as FinTech, or financial technology firms. And some of these lenders factor in where loan applicants went to college.

"It really raised some alarm flags," said Kat Welbeck, the civil rights counsel at the nonprofit Student Borrower Protection Center.

So, her group decided to run a test. It chose a lender called Upstart, in part because it's a fairly prominent fintech that says it considers educational data. And the group was able to easily apply and get loan offers on its website.

The group applied for dozens of loans online — posing as a 24-year-old man. It said he lives in New York, works as a financial analyst and makes $50,000 a year. Each time the group applied for a loan; it kept a whole range of factors constant.

"The only difference was where he went to school," Welbeck said. It applied as if this fictional borrower went to NYU in New York, many other schools and Howard University — one of the country's most famous historically Black colleges and universities.

The group found that if the otherwise identical loan applicant went to NYU instead of Howard, there was a striking difference. For a $30,000 personal loan with a five-year term, it found an applicant would pay about $3,500 more in interest and fees if they went to Howard.

"There's no other explanation that we can really come to terms with other than the fact that where this borrower went to school mattered in terms of how Upstart measured their creditworthiness," Welbeck said. And it apparently mattered quite a bit. The group also found you'd pay more if you went to New Mexico State University-Las Cruces, which has a high percentage of Hispanic students."

Surprise, surprise -- White Supremacy is still prevalent.

The new wave in politics is to support some form of marijuana legislation, either by decriminalization or in some states and localities simple legalization. On the surface, this seems like a progressive and simple thing to do. By and large, it's the right thing to do. However, a lot of people don't understand how even within this initiative, White Supremacy plays a pivotal role. One that we have to fight back on. Think about this, it's clear that people across the country in every state and in every city smoke weed. Weed isn't regulated to race, religion, income, or socioeconomic status. Both Snoop Dogg and Martha Stewart enjoy smoking weed. But if so many people do it and data is clear that the consumption is essentially equal amongst Whites and Blacks, why are Blacks arrested more for it? According to the ACLU's original analysis, marijuana arrests now account for over half of all drug arrests in the United States. Of the 8.2 million marijuana arrests between 2001 and 2010, 88% were for simply having marijuana. Nationwide, the arrest data revealed one consistent trend: significant racial bias. Despite roughly equal usage rates, Blacks are 3.73 times more likely than Whites to be arrested for marijuana.

So, what is the byproduct of said data? Well if you have a drug charge then you can't get financial aid for college. If you're already on the lower socioeconomic status side of the spectrum, how can you attend college without financial aid? If we live in a society that is adamant that people need to be credentialed with undergraduate and graduate degrees, how can a young man/woman get started if they can't afford to go to college because they did the same thing that nearly 1/2 of America has admitted to doing, but Blacks are nearly charged 4 times more than their White counterparts?

I think about one of my best friends who went to college, because that's what everyone told him he needed to do. Came home from college and tried to find a job, because that's what everyone told he needed to do. Had an entry level job making a decent salary, but the income wasn't enough because he was seen as the breadwinner in a family that sacrificed everything to pay for him to go off to school. Now that he had a job, he had to help out with his mothers' bills, his little sisters' bills, and he had young children to look after due to the homicide of his older brother. He started selling weed on the side for extra income and to help make ends meet. He never was violent, he never hurt anyone physically, he never put anyone in harm's way. One night he was caught coming back from seeing his supplier and had three pounds of weed in his trunk and $2,100 in cash in his possession. For his first offense, the judge gave him a four-year prison sentence. How do you think he feels about the fact now that people have legal weed dispensaries across the country, making the income that he was fighting for to help take care of his family, but instead of having a business in the industry, he has a felony on his record. That same friend is now 32 years old, a college degree, and is the night shift supervisor at a warehouse in Atlanta.

African Americans represent less than 1% of the total population of business owners in the cannabis industry. The industry is an estimated annual multibillion-dollar industry.

But under one in five cannabis businesses nationwide are minority-owned, according to a Marijuana Business Daily report. An August 2017 survey of 567 self-identified senior executives, owners and founders polled by the same site found that about 17% of cannabis executives were minorities. Meanwhile, a 2016 BuzzFeed analysis estimated that just 1% of 3,200 to 3,600 U.S. storefront marijuana dispensaries had Black owners.

This low participation is due in part to a lack of access to capital, advocates and entrepreneurs say. Lingering unease around the federal Schedule 1 drug poses another obstacle, advocates and entrepreneurs say: Black people are nearly four times as likely as White people to be charged with marijuana possession, despite similar usage rates, according to the American Civil Liberties Union.

As with most businesses, there is a cost to play the game. In states like Nevada, the cost for a license or permit to open up a medical marijuana dispensary is $250,000. In Washington DC, the cost for the license is in the $25,000 range. If banking institutions have shown a reluctance to lend to Black people for a variety of reasons, often rooted in racist practices and policies, then how are we supposed to gain access to this industry? When we say we need White people to use their privilege to speak up to level the playing field, this is a perfect space to do so.

In 2019, the Guardian published an article written by Sam Levin called "This was supposed to be reparations': Why is LA's cannabis industry devastating Black entrepreneurs?"

'

> *"A Los Angeles government program set up to provide cannabis licenses to people harmed by the war on drugs has been plagued by delays, scandal and bureaucratic blunders, costing some intended beneficiaries hundreds of thousands of dollars in losses.*
>
> *Black entrepreneurs and activists across LA told the Guardian that the city's embattled "social equity" program has left aspiring business owners on an indefinite waiting list, causing potentially irreparable damage to their families' finances and preventing them from opening marijuana shops they have been planning for years.*

Fewer than 20 of the 100 businesses on track to receive a license through the program appear to be Black-owned, according to estimates from advocates, who say the community most disproportionately targeted by marijuana arrests is again facing discrimination. And even some of those applicants now face precarious futures.

Meanwhile, the existing LA industry is thriving – with many White business owners at the helm.

"How do you get to come and make millions of dollars off of our misery?" said Lanaisha Edwards, a south LA native who had applied for a cannabis license through the program. "The war on drugs destroyed so many families. We should at least get to come out on the other end and create some wealth out of it. But it's not gonna happen the way this is going."

Formally launched in 2018, LA's social equity program received national attention and praise from activists as a potential model for the rest of the nation as more states move to legalize cannabis.

The city aimed to right some of the wrongs of criminalization by giving new retail licenses to people from communities historically harmed by marijuana laws, and by eliminating some of the traditional barriers in opening small businesses. Residents would be eligible if they were low-income and had cannabis arrests or convictions on their records, or lived in LA neighborhoods that were disproportionately targeted by the policing of pot.

"This was supposed to be our reparations," said Rabin Woods, 57, who was arrested in 1983 for a marijuana offense and is now struggling to open a dispensary in LA.

After California became the first state to adopt medicinal marijuana in 1996, the loosely regulated medical sector that expanded in LA and other cities largely excluded communities of color.

Out of nearly 200 cannabis retailers previously approved by the city of LA to do medical dispensaries, only six are Black-owned, according to Virgil Grant, one of the six owners and a co-founder of the California Minority Alliance, which advocates inclusion. Even fewer are Latino-owned, he said.

Residents in LA were hopeful that the social equity process, launched after the state voted to legalize recreational pot, would start to close the glaring racial gaps. But targets of the program said the process quickly became a disaster.

LA's newly formed department of cannabis regulation (DCR) first gave out licenses to businesses that were already running medical dispensaries and were considered grandfathered in under new laws. In a second round, the city doled out manufacturing and cultivation licenses for the people who wanted to legally grow cannabis.
The third phase was most critical and competitive: licensing new storefronts.
The city developed a "first-come, first-served" system for shops, and said it would give out 100 licenses to eligible social equity candidates. More than 1,800 people submitted initial applications.

When the application process officially launched on 3 September 2019, it was a high-stakes competition of who could send their online applications quickest.
"It went from social equity to who has the fastest internet," said Brandon Brinson, who applied to open a dispensary. "It was like a rat race," added Evelyn, his wife and business partner.

In December, the city admitted there were problems with the system. More than a dozen applicants had somehow received early access to the online portal. The city claimed it was a technical error that it remedied and that the mistake did not ultimately affect its consideration of applicants.

But activists and entrepreneurs cried foul, arguing it seemed the city had given some people an unfair advantage, and that the process was potentially corrupt.
The mayor ordered an "audit" of the program, and all licensing is now on hold.

In addition, many candidates who did make the top 100 list do not appear to be representative of the victims of LA's war on drugs. The eligibility requirements were not specific to race, and activists said the geographical boundaries of the impacted neighborhoods were too broad, ultimately allowing a wide range of applicants who were not directly affected by marijuana arrests.

A DCR spokesperson said the agency does not collect demographic information on business owners and is legally barred from using race as a factor in the application process. Activists estimated that only 18 of the people who made the top 100 list were African American. Some of them are still facing obstacles to launching.

In order to be eligible, the city required that applicants already possessed appropriate retail spaces, which meant many last year raced to start renting storefronts and securing investors. They are now faced with uncertain timelines and no guarantee of licenses.

Kika Keith, a leading activist for social equity applicants, who has also been trying to open her own cannabis business, has been renting a storefront in south LA for more than a year, waiting for the process to be finalized.

A single mother of three who grew up in the area where she's renting her store, Keith is exactly the kind of candidate the program was supposed to support. Her family was torn apart by criminalization, with her stepfather sentenced to five years for selling a small amount of weed: "It changed our whole lives. The psychological impact of losing him ... our whole family was disrupted. I've seen the damage." Keith planned to sell healthy infused cannabis beverages and support a youth program in the process: "My whole purpose was to reinvest in the community."

She secured the 143rd spot on the city's list, but with the uncertainty of the process and ongoing audit, her investors recently pulled out. Running out of time and money, she's now questioning whether to give up her space. "I'm starting back at point A and there's no end in sight."

Lanaisha Edwards, who was arrested for smoking pot as a teenager and had relatives spend years behind bars for marijuana offenses, had plans and a location for a Beverly Grove dispensary. It would secure financial stability for her family and emphasize healing by offering jobs for people targeted by criminalization, she said: "For my children, it would be a chance at generational wealth ... and I'd be able to give some youth employment and show that people who look like them can go into business."

At first, things look promising for Edwards, who has worked in gang intervention. She was 38th on the city's list, had already rented a location, and had the backing of an investor. But Edwards said after months of back and forth, the DCR told her she was not eligible, because her store would be located within 700ft of an "existing dispensary", violating city rules. She said the city had vetted her application, and that she had used DCR's own cannabis webpage to confirm there were no dispensaries near her space.

After researching state records, she says she discovered that DCR appeared to be allowing a marijuana shop to move in down the street from her rental because it previously had a location elsewhere in LA. The company behind it also seemed to be primarily based in Oregon. Edwards had no choice but to give up her rental after more than a year of planning.

"You jump through all of the hoops ... and it's taken away from you," she said, adding that it would be hard for would-be entrepreneurs to trust the city as the industry continued to leave people behind. "How the hell is the face of cannabis White now, how could that even be possible when you see who did all the time in jail? ... How could LA get this so wrong?"

Evelyn and Brandon Brinson, both 33, downsized their home and sold a car to finance their planned marijuana business. Evelyn also sold an insurance agency she had run, and Brandon who is a barber, stopped paying rent for space at a shop. "Our whole life savings are in this project," said Evelyn.

On a recent afternoon, the couple showed the Guardian around the still vacant store they had rented to house their dispensary. They pointed to empty glass shelves and the display counters that would feature their products. They estimate they have lost more than $200,000 on the endeavor. Their application is number 200 on the list, and they don't think they can hold on much longer.

"Why call it social equity and make people think that you're

helping the Black and brown communities?" Evelyn said. "It's stressful seeing everything that you've worked for in your entire life being placed in something that you thought was going to be an opportunity to help you and it has literally hurt you."

Evelyn and Brandon co-own their business with Rayford Brown, a 57-year old LA resident who served a five-year sentence for a marijuana offense. He was wary from the beginning that the same government that locked him up to "teach him a lesson" when he was homeless and occasionally "selling weed to eat" would now want to help him be a legal marijuana entrepreneur.

"What is your actual objective in giving me a 'second chance'? You have this cannabis industry that you consider the 'right way', but when I was convicted, there was no right way," he said. "It's absolutely amazing that we are even at this point where we're literally fighting and waiting for approval from a state that convicted me and wanted to give me five years for the first time in my life over weed."

Kika Keith, the activist who has been trying to open a cannabis business in south LA, said she was not ready to give up, and she would not stop advocating for others.

"This is for my children, but there is a bigger legacy beyond my own family. We are dealing with a multibillion-dollar industry that by no means wants us in it. It's important for us to fight for our position in this industry."

So, let's put this into perspective, Black folk are four times more likely to be arrested for marijuana. Represent less than 13% of the total United States population but nearly 40% of the prison population. Black people represent less than 1% of the ownership in the marijuana industry, and what was once something that brothers and sisters were sentenced to multiple years in prison for, is now a billion-dollar industry with White people getting grants and government funding to open up? James Baldwin said it best, "To be a Negro in this country and to be relatively conscious is to be in a rage almost all the time."

I often think back to the feeling that rushed through my body on my 21st birthday in Orangeburg, South Carolina. It was Tuesday, November 4,' 2008. My friends had a party for me at a local bar and lounge across the street from campus. Everyone who knows me, knows that I don't drink alcohol, and tonight was no different. College can be filled with peer pressure to consume as much alcohol as possible on days that many consider to be milestones. My focus was on something else though. Tonight was the night that Barack Hussein Obama was elected to the office of President of the United States. I've always had an affinity for changing my community. I never knew exactly what I wanted to do, or how I wanted to do it, but tonight was the night that I knew that one day I would run for office. Fast forward seven years later, November 4, 2015 (yes, on my birthday), I officially won my election to the Charlottesville City Council. The feeling of pride. The feeling of joy. The responsibility of doing what was necessary to improve my community was a responsibility that I was ready for. However, as I look back on both points of my life. There are a few things that stick out.

While Barack Obama became the first African American to win either the Democratic or Republican nomination, to do so, he had to be what I like to call "Super Negro." In order to become president, Barack had to have a resume that was essentially impeccable, a story that was beyond compelling, a level of intellect that was beyond reproach, and a look and tone of voice that made the majority of Americans (i.e. White people) comfortable. Obama was the son of parents from Kenya and Kansas. He was born in Kansas and raised in Hawaii. He graduated from two Ivy League schools, Columbia for undergrad, and Harvard Law for graduate school. He was the first Black person to serve as President of the Harvard Law Review. He was a community organizer in Chicago, worked at one of the most prestigious law firms in the city, was a state senator, U.S. Senator, and essentially all of this is what laid the path to the Presidency. His immediate successor, Donald John Trump, was the son of a millionaire real estate agent. Both had been sued multiple times for racial discrimination. Trump has been accused of sexual assault countless times, filed for bankruptcy multiple times, for college, Trump studied two years at New York City's Fordham University then transferred to the University of Pennsylvania's Wharton School of Finance and Commerce, where he earned an undergraduate degree in 1968. During the Vietnam War, he received four student deferments and one medical deferment and wasn't drafted for military service. He also is the same person that took out a full-page ad calling for the death penalty of the Central Park 5. Before running for president of the United States, he had no political experience, nor had he ever ran for or won a political election on any level. Does anyone notice a difference in the two?

I remember feeling in my own election that things were different. I knew I was qualified, but I was aiming to become only the seventh Black person ever elected to the City Council of a city that was founded in 1762. I was more than qualified from an educational perspective, as I had two degrees at the time. I had been a high school educator for several years. I ran a boxing club for underprivileged youth in the city. I supplied around 200 turkeys every Thanksgiving to families. I provided nearly 300 coats every Christmas for those in need. I worked to distribute school supplies and backpacks before every school year. I memorized the city budget inside and out. I knew the policies inside and out. I was more than prepared to lead the city – however, I was consistently questioned about my experience to take on such a *big* job. I was consistently reminded by people in the city that I wasn't from Charlottesville. In comparison, the guy who ended up winning the election in 2013 had fewer degrees than I did, had run for office three or four times, switched parties a couple of times, presented no policy ideas during his campaign, brought forth few tangible ideas about how to make the city a better place, but yet he still won. Now, I am not saying that he was a bad person, and we actually got along very well after I won my election in 2015, but this experience was a prime example of what my grandmother would say to me on a regular basis. "We" have to be twice as good as the White folks to get anything in this country. She was right in more ways than one. White Supremacy doesn't just make White people question the worth, value, and preparedness of Black candidates; it makes a lot of Black people also feel as if other Black people have to be "Super Negro" in order to serve in positions of leadership. I have seen countless instances in which Black people will hold Black candidates to a standard that they wouldn't think about having for a White candidate. In the 2019-2020 election cycle, it was absolutely sickening to see the things that people would say about Presidential candidate Kamala Harris regarding her record as a prosecutor in California all while allowing the author of Stop and Frisk to get a pass and earn their support. It was incredibly disappointing to see people give disparaging remarks about the "Blackness" of Cory Booker, a Black man, while simultaneously giving Joe Biden, Bernie Sanders, Elizabeth Warren, and "Mayor Pete" an invitation to the proverbial cookout. While I am not saying that any of the aforementioned White people are bad folks, what I do find disappointing was how quickly some of us will turn on our own for what we believe to be "greener pastures." Repeatedly I have seen us believe the worst about each other (even when it's not true), spread misinformation about each other, and give other people the benefit of the doubt when they make similar mistakes.

It is common practice for Black folk to be incredibly hard on other Black folk in leadership. This, in my opinion, is not only a byproduct of White Supremacy, but furthermore a symptom on what Dr. Joy DeGrue has labeled *Post Traumatic Slave Syndrome*.

PTSS is a theory that explains the etiology for many of the adaptive survival behaviors in African American communities throughout the United States and the Diaspora. It is a condition that exists as a consequence of multigenerational oppression of Africans and their descendants resulting from centuries of chattel slavery. A form of slavery which was predicated on the belief that African Americans were inherently/genetically inferior to Whites. This was then followed by institutionalized racism, which continues to perpetuate injury.

*Thus, resulting in **M.A.P.**:*

- ☐ ***M:*** *Multigenerational trauma together with continued oppression;*

- ☐ ***A:*** *Absence of opportunity to heal or access the benefits available in the society; leads to*

- ☐ ***P:*** *Post Traumatic Slave Syndrome.*

    Under such circumstances these are some of the predictable patterns of behavior that tend to occur:

KEY PATTERNS OF BEHAVIOR REFLECTIVE OF PTSS

Vacant Esteem
Insufficient development of what Dr. DeGruy refers to as primary esteem, along with feelings of hopelessness, depression and a general self-destructive outlook.

Marked Propensity for Anger and Violence *Extreme feelings of suspicion perceived negative motivations of others. Violence against self, property and others, including the members of one's own group, i.e. friends, relatives, or acquaintances.*

Racist Socialization and (internalized racism)

Learned Helplessness, literacy deprivation, distorted self-concept, antipathy or aversion for the following:

☐ *The members of one's own identified cultural/ethnic group,*

☐ *The mores and customs associated with one's own identified cultural/ethnic heritage,*

☐ *The physical characteristics of one's own identified cultural/ethnic group.*

Unfortunately, a lot of us don't even realize that we are suffering from PTSS, and subsequently, we refuse to support each other politically, educationally, economically, and emotionally, because we have been conditioned to not value, respect, or love each other. Again, white supremacy is not regulated to just white people. A lot of black people share the same views about other black people as some white supremacists. Their covert and overt prejudice comes out subconsciously. However, although white supremacy has done a number on our society as a whole, it does not mean that it has to prevail. We, all of us, have the ability to unite, stand tall together, and continue to defeat it. It is hard, yes, but if it was easy, it wouldn't be as fun.

8 TALKING WHITE, TALKING BLACK, TALKING YOURSELF

The English language and the different variations of such have been around for thousands of years. What we say, how we say it, the tone that we use, and the context in which we say things has been a point of contention for generations. Whether we want to admit it or not, the way in which people speak is often tied to how they are viewed in society. I have been an avid reader since I was in the 5th or 6th grade, and because of such, my vocabulary has been rather expansive. I can't tell you how many times I've been told "You speak so well." Or the infamous, "You are so articulate." It often feels like people are utterly shocked that someone who is Black can speak in a way in which they deem "proper." This isn't regulated to just White people saying this to me. While it may be surprising to a lot of people who don't look like me, it has been my experience that a lot of Black people are often shocked when one of us has a command of the English language. From as a child, to a teenager, to college student, to young adult, to fully grown man, the way in which I use words has always either raised eye brows of some, made some people ask silly questions, or as of late, cause a juxtaposition that leaves some confused. In more recent years, regardless of the political position that I may hold, or the level of education that I have, I dress in a way that *some* deem as unbecoming or that does not fit with said position or education level. I will never forget appearing on CNN shortly after the tragic White supremacist attacks to Charlottesville in August of 2017. I remember intentionally not wearing a suit on the day of August 12, but wearing a pair of Air Max 95s, Levi Jeans, a shirt that read "Menace II Supremacy" which was a play on words paying homage to John Singleton's movie "Menace II Society", two gold chains, and my earrings. I was standing directly behind Governor McAuliffe as he addressed the nation condemning the attacks, with my same clothes on while others were either in their suits or police uniforms. I was comfortable with being myself, and more importantly, I wanted to send a message that this is also what leadership looks like. My resilience, my desire for change, my push to make things better was not predicated based on the clothes that I had on. As I had my own interview on CNN later that evening, I spoke with conviction about the need for our community to stand strong, fight off White Supremacy, and call on people to fight in unison against the bigotry and hate that we endured earlier that day. My words were poignant, and my attire was "different" which subsequently became a topic of conversation. As the days went on, and more and more came out about the background of our city, I was in the national media more. I would sometimes wear a suit, but I would also sometimes wear t-shirts that had a message on them. What I wore was all based on how I felt at the time. Subsequently, I was approached on several occasions by different people about the way I dressed on television. A few elders in the community attempted to pull me to the side, to tell me how much they enjoyed seeing me represent the city on the national level, but could I put a suit on and take my earrings out the next time that I went on? I expected this from the trolls online who called me all kinds of "thug", "Nigger", or some other derogatory term. To be honest, it wasn't surprising that some of the elders were more concerned with how I dressed and presented myself opposed to what I was actually saying/doing. I was also expecting most young people to tell me that they felt inspired by what they believed was a level of authenticity from an elected official. While this feels good, it also makes me ponder how low is the bar? There isn't a week that doesn't go by in which someone doesn't come up to me and say something to the effect of "I love how you talk. You articulate so well." While I appreciate the love and the compliments, it often leaves me wondering, what did you expect me to do? Go on television and pontificate in a manner that would make you ashamed? On a more critical thinking scale, is the bar for our people set so low that the expectation or the norm is for us to appear on national settings or media outlets and speak in a way in which our family members would be ashamed?

Some will say that this simply shows a lack of expectations amongst some people, others will say things like there is a generational divide. Others will say this is simply a byproduct of culture. A few will chalk this up to simply, this is how people are. All of this may be true; however, I would like to challenge each person reading this to go deeper and think about *who* set the *norms* for our society? Furthermore, whom or what as a society, has made some people believe what is and what is not appropriate, proper, and who is allowed and not allowed to operate in such as their norm?

This issue around what some people consider to be appropriate in comparison to not appropriate is one that must be explored when discussing White Supremacy. Appropriateness, specifically as it pertains to language, diction, enunciation, and so forth is a byproduct of White Supremacy in more ways than one. Whether we want to admit it or not, a lot of people across the globe, and more specifically in the United States of America, equate speaking in a way that displays an extensive vocabulary or showing a command of the current English language as a form of Whiteness. It is almost as if, speaking "well" or using certain words are only for people from affluent backgrounds or upbringings, and in our society, more often than not, those people have been White.

"Man, this nigga over here talking like a White boy. Using all those big words and shit. Talk regular bruh, talk like you Black."

"Wesley, you do know that it's ok to talk Black right? You ain't around those White people. You ain't at a meeting, you can talk regular." I can personally say that I learned very early on, as in Kindergarten, that different people deserved different conversations. Much of this was due to the fact that I was born in Myrtle Beach, South Carolina and spent most of my time in Atlantic Beach, South Carolina. Atlantic Beach, aka, the Black Pearl was the epicenter for Black culture in the region. I went to pre-school in this community. I learned to read at the daycare in this community, watched my family and their friends hustle in this community, was told that I was special and was going to be somebody in this community, and also was told, "Stop talking and acting like a White boy" for the first time in my life in this community. After my mother and I moved to Atlanta, I was already well equipped in code-switching, which led to me becoming a leader at an early age. I had an affinity for reading, an affinity for helping people, and I was consistently told that I was special, which led to me wanting to fulfill the prophecy that was placed on my life at an early age.

While all of this was true, I grew up around Black people, low income Black people at that. As much as I was told that I was special, I also noticed that other kids at school or in our neighborhood who talked about reading, or science, or soccer instead of basketball were consistently told "Stop acting White." To be clear, whether my friends and family realized it or not, what they were deeming to be regular was actually "African American Vernacular English" (yes, there is a term for it) and not "standard English." African American Vernacular English, also known as AAVE, has a distinct place in American history. What some people see as broken English, Ebonics, or just talking "Black" is much deeper than what the surface may show. To break this down in Layman's Terms, AAVE is a variety of language spoken predominately by members of the African American or Black race in America, although White people speak it too. It is distinct from general American English, as AAVE has its own sound, its own diction, vocabulary, and its own grammar. While the original origin of AAVE cannot be pinpointed, most researchers and scholars agree that it began as the enslaved Africans came over to the "New World", and was created as a way for the enslaved to communicate with each other and the White people who now appointed themselves as their "masters".

This theory makes sense, as it is common knowledge that the enslaved Africans who arrived in America were from different families, tribes, villages, towns, cities, and countries for that matter. While most enslaved Africans were thrust into situations in which they knew very few people from their native land or spoke their native tongue, they had to discover a way to be able to communicate with each other. In many ways, it was a survival tactic. Some scholars believe that subsequently they created what was known as "pidgin English". Within a couple of generations, this "Pidgin English" developed into what was later known as creoles, or in some circles "Geechie" or "Gullah". These creoles were eventually blended into other forms of English as the enslaved spent more time with the slavers, and as the language developed, different forms of the creole also developed and manifested into what we hear today. It has been stated that over time the creole was decreolized, it was put into more simpler forms until we got to what we have today, AAVE. For others, AAVE is not actually a language, but instead a dialect.

While writing for dictionary.com, Taneesh Khera eloquently explained the difference between the two.

"If you call it a dialect, *you support the* Anglicist Hypothesis *that African slaves on Southern plantations acquired English from their British owners. This hypothesis was the widely held opinion of how AAVE evolved until the 1960s. If you say it's a* language, *though, you hold the* Creolist Hypothesis *view, that AAVE originated from a creole spoken on Southern plantations before the Civil War. A* creole *is a full language that develops from a pidgin, a super simple language created between two groups who need to communicate but don't have a language in common. Linguists of this view say AAVE arose from a creole*

in West Africa that slaves already spoke before coming to the US.

Scholars still argue about what AAVE should be called, leaning one way or another at different times. In fact, in 1996 the school board in Oakland, California proactively, and unanimously, believed the Creolist view. After three hours of hearing the arguments, the board revised literature to explicitly call AAVE a distinct language from SAE, recognizing it as the native language of around 30,000 African American students within the school district."

While our enslaved ancestors had to learn a new way to communicate with each other and their oppressor to survive, they also had to adapt to a new way of life and culture. Code switching is a term that is often thrown around today to describe, as Carlos Morrison of the Britannica Encyclopedia wrote, "The process of shifting from one linguistic code (a language or dialect) to another, depending on the social context or conversational setting." The argument can be made that in America, the enslaved Africans were one of the first groups of people to have to do so for survival. Native Americans had their land ravished, they were brutally murdered, and subsequently forced out of the very place that they lived for thousands of years. This was (and still is) home for the Indigenous population, so code switching to make other people feel welcomed was not something that was too common during the early years of America. However, for enslaved Africans, this territory was new. It was foreign. The rules were different, and the consequences could literally be life or death. What some people now view as the enslaved devaluing themselves, or "shucking and Jiving" was nothing more than code switching for survival. It is well documented how many enslaved Africans despised their masters and defied them in subtle, covert, and overt ways. However, one cannot blame someone, during that particular era, for doing what they must in order to survive. Instead, I think about how treacherous and evil some White people must have been during that era to make other human beings endure such treatment. What is even more unfortunate, for many, both society and some Black people, it is *still* important for Black folk to code switch to survive in the same systems that were built by White Supremacy.

Carlos Morrison further elaborates on code switching and its origin writing:

> *"Sociolinguists, social psychologists, and identity researchers are interested in the ways in which code-switching, particularly by members of minority ethnic groups, is used to shape and maintain a sense of identity and a sense of belonging to a larger community. In the United States, code-switching was originally studied in the context of second-language acquisition as the process whereby native speakers of Spanish shifted from Spanish to English and vice versa. Code-switching was also studied among African Americans who shifted between standard English (a dialect of English that is recognized as the national norm in the United States and is spoken or written by the educated classes) and African American English (AAE), an Africanized dialect widely spoken by Americans of African descent. Other terms for African American English are African American Language, African American Vernacular English, Black English, Standard Black English, and Ebonics.*

> *Code-switching among African American students has been recognized since the 1970s and has informed different views of those students' home dialect (AAE) and different approaches to the teaching of standard English. The "correctionist" approach to code-switching suggests that the students' home speech amounts to "broken English" or "poor grammar." Correctionists may also apply derogatory labels such as "ghetto" or "country." From the perspective of the correctionist, if the students' home speech is broken, then it needs to be corrected by getting*

them to use the appropriate language—standard English. For the correctionist, the students' home speech is nothing more than a set of bad habits that prevent them from mastering correct English.

According to American linguists Benjamin Lee Whorf and Edward Sapir, language has the power to shape the worldview and identity of its users. Both the correctionist and contrastivist ideologies shape, through language, the identities of students in uniquely different ways. The student whose language is shaped by the correctionist's ideology may adopt a mainstream cultural identity, one that is couched in Eurocentric values, ideals, and customs.

However, the student whose language is shaped by the contrastivist's ideology may adopt different cultural identities depending on the social context or conversational setting. Here, the speaker may move back and forth between the dialect of the dominant culture and the home dialect, depending on the situation. So, for example, an African American business executive addressing colleagues in a professional setting may express disapproval by saying "I disagree." However, the same individual, addressing friends in an informal setting, may say, "That ain't cool." It is safe to say that many African Americans, particularly within the middle class, speak on a continuum ranging from the language of the suites to the language of the streets." - Carlos D. Morrison – Code-Switching published in the online Encyclopedia Britannica.

You Aren't Good Enough as You Are, so be Someone Else.

Take a moment to think about that, or that experience as a young person, young adult, grown man or woman, and on a deeper level, generations as a whole. The thought that the way in which you are, in your natural state is not good enough. The fact of the matter is that a lot of White people do not have to operate or navigate in systems in which they don't have to be anyone except for the people that they have always been. Some White people willingly ignore the fact that some people have literally been forced to enter into a country or land in which their native tongue was shunned, they were beaten and in some cases physically killed for trying to maintain their language and traditions Furthermore, the only way to be seen as somewhat more than the person who looked like them who had been categorized as a wild beast, the same level as cattle, and most importantly 3/5 of a human being, was to learn to speak, act, and make White people feel at ease. This way of thinking has been passed down from generation to generation, and in many ways still at play today. Code switching can be an excruciating act. If you think this is challenging, navigating the social scene in a world in which few people look like you, imagine not being able to be yourself around other Black people who look like you, have had to endure the same struggle as you, and have had to live in the same systems as you. This is the reality for a lot of people who identify as Black in America, and elsewhere. We live in a society that is based on White standards, yet our measures of Blackness is often questioned by ourselves, and in some cases, we give other people who aren't Black to question our credence of Blackness based on the standard that they have seen on television or even worse, social media. While it has never been my personal experience, I have several friends who have spoken at length with me about the pain of being called "Oreo" (Black on the outside and White on the inside) while growing up. The pain of being told that they aren't Black enough, or other painful epithets being thrown at them throughout their childhood, teenage years, and even as adults. I posed the question on my Instagram story on one Sunday Afternoon "Any of my Black followers ever been accused of talking or acting White?" "If yes, how did this make you feel?" The responses were heartbreaking, but unfortunately not surprising. Things like:

"It left me feeling that I wasn't 'Black' enough."

"Less Black, like I needed to change the way I talk to be considered Black"

"Like Black people can't sound any other way except for ghetto or uneducated"

"Minimized, sometimes, tokenized, depending on who said it"

Two of the most consistent responses were:
"hurt" and **"confused"**

If we are being authentic with ourselves, we will admit that for both Black and White people, the belief that White is right is the standard that has been set by a society that is rooted in White Supremacy. If we are also being truthful, many of us, both Black and White, have been conditioned to believe that this standard is the one that we must operate in if we are going to be successful in life. Anything that deviates outside of this standard is cause for us to believe that whatever is seen as different will not be successful. The juxtaposition that comes with the standard of Whiteness that has been set by White Supremacy is extremely complex. On one hand, the standard is that success is on par with Whiteness, but Whiteness is also frowned upon in many respects, and subsequently being identified with such can lead to ridicule.

This often makes me think of what I almost always here every Black person running for political office say while they are campaigning. The infamous line that comes in the variation of "I don't want you to vote for me because I am Black. I want you to vote for me because I am the best person for the job." Think about that for a second. Can you ever recall a Jewish American saying, "I don't want you to vote for me, because I am a Jew, I want you to vote for me because I am the best person for the job"? Have you ever heard an Irish American running for any political office say, "I don't want your vote just because I am Irish, I want your vote because I am the most qualified person for this seat?" Or think as far back as you can and think of someone who identifies as White speaking about their race in a way that challenges people to see past their race and vote for them based on their merits. We all would be hard pressed to find such examples. Why? The answer is simple. The playing field for Black people and other people in our society is different. Ok, that is not something that is new, but the fact that we can pretend that it is normal is the issue. The larger issue is that far too many Black people believe that they have to decrease themselves in these kinds of settings to get a vote. This is beyond troubling. Yes, troubling for voters, and excruciating for the actual candidate. I vividly remember being a young man running for the Charlottesville City Council and my advisors saying to me as clear as day "Wes, I know you spend a lot of time in the low income and public housing neighborhoods, but you are going to have to broaden your base if you want to win a city wide election. The people who are in those neighborhoods don't always vote, and you can't rely on them to win. If you are going to branch out into the other neighborhoods, you are going to have to switch up your message. You are going to have to become more polished. You are going to have to change." So I did just that, I often changed my vernacular according to who I was speaking with, I immersed myself into topics that didn't necessarily have an impact on the people that I interacted with on a day to day basis, and I began to speak in a tone that was less aggressive, dressed in a way that put more people at ease, and I communicated in a way that put people at ease. I was the only African American in the race, and the city didn't have any Black people on the city council, however I had to reiterate at almost every campaign event that I didn't want to be elected because I was the only person who was Black in the race, but I wanted their vote because I was the best candidate. The fallacy in this was that I had to sacrifice who I truly was in order to get a position to help the community. In the eyes of the voters, I was evolving as a young man before their very eyes. While this was indeed true, the fact also remained that I was playing the proverbial "game" and doing what I had to in order to get the seat that I wanted. In reality, I was the only person in the city council race who could relate to our low-income community, to our Black community, to the people who didn't usually come to the city council meetings, and to a large sector of our city who was underrepresented. Why was I not allowed to be explicit in that regard? Why could I not be the best candidate and the person who could reach out to this population that had a void in representation? In turn, what was the reward for me not being so explicit? I won all ten precincts in the election and was the leading vote getter.

The same logic applies for the Black man or woman who is attempting to climb the corporate ladder. The one young man who believes that he has to dress a certain way, speak a certain way, and endure a racial slur or generalization about Black people while being told he's "not like the others" while at work. It's similar for the Black woman who consistently has jokes told about her hair or endures micro-aggressions on a daily and has to do her best to quell her emotions because the moment that she responds she will be known as the "Angry Black woman." Tami Winfrey Harris eloquently explains in her 2010 article entitled, "What's So Wrong With "Sounding Black?"

"The multilingualism required to speak one way to a Southern grandmother, another way to youths raised on MTV, and still another way in a corporate boardroom can be as challenging as learning to juggle three balls without dropping one. It can lead to the painful "yo-yo effect," as a woman feels conflicted about shifting between two distinct voices, self-conscious about using the "wrong" voice in the wrong situation. Women who have difficulty switching may be mocked or unfairly criticized by Blacks and Whites alike. "She thinks she's White." "She tries too hard to sound Black." "She's a ghetto girl." "She's not very bright."

African Americans face a conundrum, then. Black vernacular English is unacceptable. Standard English spoken with an accent common to Black Americans is unacceptable. And being able to move smoothly between the speech patterns of the Black community and those of the broader White community is suspicious. What is so wrong about "sounding Black?" The answer should be "nothing at all."

Having to quell who you really are to make other people feel comfortable can be painful. For that very reason, there are people who refuse to code switch. There is a growing community, that many will argue has been in existence for generations, who refuse to downplay their expansive vocabulary, change the diction within their voice, or shy away from their passion for academia to make others feel comfortable. This particular group of Black people fight White Supremacy by simply being themselves, and not changing for the others. Those "others" can be both either Black or White. My Charlottesville neighbor and New York Times journalist Jamelle Bouie wrote a phenomenal article a few years ago about

Talking White

Black people's disdain for "proper English" and academic achievement is a myth.

By JAMELLE BOUIE

A 2005 study found that "Black adolescents are generally achievement oriented and that racialized peer pressure against high academic achievement is not prevalent in all schools."

"All right, hear me out," begins the young Black woman in a video uploaded to the website LiveLeak last Friday. "There is no such thing as 'talking White,' ... it's actually called 'speaking fluently,' speaking your language correctly. I don't know why we've gotten to a place where as a culture—as a race—if you sound as though you have more than a fifth-grade education, it's a bad thing."

She continues like this for nearly two more minutes, emphasizing the point that her speech reflects proper English and attacking the idea that it's a deviation from Black identity.

If she was hoping for a positive response, she got it. In addition to thousands of shares and tweets, it reached more than 560,000 views and made the front page of Reddit.

Not that this was a surprise. The main ideas—that Black Americans disparage "proper English" and education and use a "broken" version of the language—have wide currency among many Americans, including Blacks.

"Ebonics" is mocked as a fake language, and efforts to use it in schools have sparked vocal opposition. When the Oakland, California, school board approved Ebonics for use in its schools in 1996, a flurry of public figures condemned the decision. "I understand the attempt to reach out to these children, but this is an unacceptable surrender, bordering on disgrace," said the Rev. Jesse Jackson, who later reversed his stance, but not before he was endorsed by a wide range of people.

At the time, linguists protested the criticism, noting the extent to which Ebonics—officially known as African American Vernacular English—is recognized as a language system with its own grammar and pronunciations, with roots in the regional dialects of 17th-century Great Britain. Far from being slang or broken, AAVE is a distinct form of English used by many Blacks in informal settings.

Still, it is true that so-called "proper English"—otherwise known as Standard English—is associated with White people. And there are many anecdotes and stories of Black teenagers disparaging one another for using Standard English or "talking White," which also tends to come with accusations of "acting White." And, as we can see from the video, it's these accusations that stand as Exhibit A in arguments for the existence of Black pathology.

After relating a story involving his sister and her children, who asked him why he "talk White," Wall Street Journal columnist Jason Riley mourns the alleged pathology of Black anti-intellectualism that stunts community growth. "Here were a couple of Black third graders already linking speech patterns to race and intelligence," he writes in his book Please Stop Helping Us. "They had determined that 'sounding White' was something to be mocked in other Blacks and avoided in their own speech."

In this anecdote, Riley provides the nut of the "acting White" theory: That Blacks stigmatize academic achievement and code it as "White." But as he notes in the book, the definitive treatment comes from the late John Ogbu, a professor of anthropology at the University of California–Berkeley.

In multiple studies over several decades, Ogbu explored the allegedly "oppositional" culture of Black teenagers and pushed the "acting White" idea into the popular discourse. "The low school performance of Black children stems from the following factors," he writes with Signithia Fordham in the 1986 paper, "Black Students' School Success: Coping with the Burden of 'Acting White' ":

First, White people provide them with inferior schooling and treat them differently in school; second, by imposing a job ceiling, White people fail to reward them adequately for their educational achievements in adult life; and third, Black Americans develop coping mechanisms which, in turn, further limit their striving for academic success.

Ogbu was thorough and convincing enough to spawn a whole genre of popular work around "acting White." Besides Riley, the most recent contributions include Ron Christie's Acting White: The Curious History of a Racial Slur and Stuart Buck's Acting White: The Ironic Legacy of Desegregation, which—like Ogbu's work— argues that Blacks lag in educational outcomes because of a cultural bias against academic achievement.

In the last 10 years, however, new research has challenged the "acting White" theory. In a 2005 paper, sociologists Karolyn Tyson, William Darity Jr., and Domini Castellino found "that Black adolescents are generally achievement oriented and that racialized peer pressure against high academic achievement is not prevalent in all schools."

According to their research—drawn from interviews with students across eight North Carolina schools—racialized stigma against high achievement exists. But it requires specific circumstances, namely, predominantly White schools where few Blacks attend advanced classes. There, Black and White students hold racialized perceptions of educational achievement, and Black students are often isolated by stigma from both groups. As one school counselor notes:

They did not like being in honors courses because often they were the only ones. ... Also, some of the kids felt that if they were in these honors classes, that their peers, the Black kids look at them as if they were acting White, not recognizing that you could be smart and Black. A lot of White kids look at them, basically, "You're not supposed to be smart and Black, so why are you here?"

By contrast, "acting White" accusations were least common at the most segregated schools, a finding echoed by a 2006 study from Harvard economist Roland Fryer, who found "no evidence at all that getting good grades adversely affects students' popularity" in predominantly Black schools.

Across schools, the general pattern was this: "Acting White" accusations weren't attached to academic performance and rather were a function of specific behaviors. If you hung out with White kids and adopted White fashions, you were accused of "acting White." Smart kids were teased, but no more than you'd see in any other group.

Indeed, one of the most fascinating observations from Tyson, Darity, and Castellino was the extent to which an anti-intellectual culture existed among Whites as well:

[C]ontrary to the implications of the burden of acting White and oppositional peer culture hypotheses—that White students generally have superior standards for academic achievement and are embedded in peer groups that support and encourage

129

academic striving—the experiences described by some of our White [student] informants indicate the presence of a much less achievement-oriented academic culture.

In interviews, White students describe ostracism from peers and apprehension from parents who want to avoid the perception of "elitism" that comes with children in gifted programs.

Again, none of this is to deny the reality of racialized ridiculing. It happens—I've experienced it—and it's painful. But it isn't a feature of Black culture. Rather, it arises from a mix of factors, from social status to the composition of the school itself. As the sociologists note in their conclusion, stigmatization for Whites and Blacks seemed to come from the "perception that the low-status student was attempting to assume the characteristic of the 'other,' especially an air of superiority or arrogance."

With all of that said, let's circle back to the video. "I don't know why we've gotten to a place whereas a culture—as a race—if you sound as though you have more than a fifth-grade education, it's a bad thing," says the woman. Ignore the mistaken attack on African American Vernacular English. Knowing what we now know about "acting White," we should read this complaint in a different light.

If her peers have mocked her for "talking White," it might have less to do with her use of Standard English overall and more to do with its use in an unusual setting. Remember, for many Americans, Standard English is only used in formal settings—business and school, but not home. By forgoing the vernacular in informal speech, she might come across as elitist, in the same way it might seem pretentious to purposefully use professional jargon when talking with a non-specialist.

In other words, she isn't being mocked for the English as much as she is for her refusal to code-switch and use informal language for an informal conversation. That might be unfair—let's say you can't actually speak the vernacular!—but it's not evidence of pathology.

Or, as a teacher might tell her students, there's language for home, and there's language for school, and sometimes, what works for one place might not work for the other."

Again, code switching is a sport that Black folk have had to play as a means of survival for generations. However, wouldn't life be better if our White allies recognized the role that they play in these games of advancement, and subsequently cut it short? Wouldn't it be better if White people used their voice and privilege so that Black people could be free to wear what they want, speak however they like, and campaign in whatever way made them feel comfortable? Wouldn't it better if Black people as a whole loved ourselves to allow ourselves to speak however we wanted without condemnation? Wouldn't it be beautiful if Black people loved each other and ourselves to not worry about what other people think about us? White Supremacy knocks daily in this regard, do you answer the door and fight back? Or do you usher it in and remain silent as it runs rampant throughout your surroundings?

9. FORGIVENESS, CHRISTIANITY, AND WHITE SUPREMACY

"A lot of Black people don't want to be on the wrong side of God."
– KJ Kearney

I sat in a movie theater crying like a newborn, mainly because I felt every single emotion that Jackie Robinson felt during this particular scene of the movie "42." After being called a Nigger, being berated, being treated like an animal during a baseball game, and treated with less dignity than a stray dog during his tenure breaking the color barrier in major sports, Jackie Robinson reached his breaking point. He went into the hallway of the dugout and let out a scream from the depth and pit of his soul. He broke his baseball bat into several pieces while screaming, yelling, crying, and letting it all out. He let it all out alone. None of his teammates came to console him. There was nobody who came to his rescue. In fact, the team owner saw him in the hallway, and told him he had to have the courage and the dignity to *not* fight back. That my friends, is one aspect of the Black experience in a country and society that is predicated around a religion that was used to keep people who look like myself and Jackie in bondage, but still want us to navigate and push through.

I grew up in the church, as religion, and specifically Christianity is embedded in me and is a part of my DNA and human fabric as much as the color of my skin. I was born in South Carolina, grew up in Atlanta, and went back to South Carolina to finish high school and subsequently attend college. I grew up spending most of my Sundays in church. Faithfully, if it was Sunday, my grandmother or aunt(s) had me in church. I wasn't always the most well-behaved young man, and my family enjoys telling the story of my paternal grandmother, Evie Mae, giving me a few licks to my backside one Sunday afternoon for misbehaving inside of Atlantic Beach Missionary Baptist Church. While my father's side of the family may have been known for other extra-curricular activities, my grandmother made sure that my foundation was rooted in the church. On my mothers' side of the family, religion plays such a significant role, that at least ten members of the immediate family were and still are pastors, preachers, deacons, musicians, or played

a significant role in the church. My maternal great-grandmother,

MeMe, also made sure that "Web" (as she was too old to pronounce "Wes") was at church. While living in Atlanta, one of my earliest memories was my little brother Javin, who was a newborn at the time, crying inside of Central Baptist Church (the old little church – those from the Central know exactly what I mean) and the

Pastor, Pastor Kimble, saying during his sermon, "Young lady, that baby crying does us no harm here. That baby is also waiting to hear from the Lord. It is all right. Let the baby cry." I remember thinking, wow. That was amazing. This pastor is really nice. I remember going on my first Missions trip with that same church when I was 12 years old to Matamoras, Mexico, and that same pastor saying, "The guest church wants someone from the youth group to give a speech tonight. I will help you with it, but we need someone to do it. Who wants to do it?" And out of nowhere, my hand raised. He later told me, "I knew it was going to be you." I remember my church allowing me to have 10 minutes in front of the entire congregation once a month to practice my public speaking skills. I remember them allowing me to come back while I was in college and give an actual sermon. I remember thinking throughout all of my life that my God, will never leave me. My God will never forsake me. I've been in neighborhood shootouts, caught in the crossfire of attempts on my life, dealt with depression, White supremacists trying to take my life, my family's life, and been the target of all kinds of hate. It has been my faith and belief in God that has always pushed me through. This religion that has saved my life, this religion that has spoken to me during my darkest times, is the same religion that a lot of people use to keep my people in a state of being docile.

Christianity, and the way in which some people interpret the religion as a whole, may be the biggest proprietor of White Supremacy in history. This country's fundamental values and laws are built on Christianity, and this same Christianity has in its holy book,

"Slaves, obey your earthly masters with respect and fear, and with sincerity of heart, just as you would obey Christ." - Ephesians 6:5 New International Version (NIV).

As my ancestors had unborn fetuses ripped out of their wombs. As my ancestors had their children ripped from the tight holds of mothers who didn't want their sons and daughters sold off.

As my ancestors were mutilated.

As my ancestors were raped.

As my ancestors had their hands, feet, legs, eyes, and genitals cut off.

As my ancestors had their backs beaten to the point of the mere sight would make the toughest man cry.

As my ancestors had their native tongues figuratively and literally ripped out of their mouths.

As my ancestors were told, mostly by their masters, and the other Blacks that they brainwashed, that their reward would be in Heaven, and if they did not obey their master, they surely were going to Hell.

Christianity has played a significant role in American history, and there is no denying the impact that it has had on race relations in America. From past to present, not one soul who is willing to be honest with themselves can deny how the institution of Christianity, the business of Christianity, and the belief by some

White people that God created them to be superior to others, has had a negative impact on race relations in our country.

Kevin Powell wrote in 2019 about the *Insanity of White Justice and Black Forgiveness*:

"There is no way to discuss America, its history, even the very nature of its democracy, without also discussing race, racism, and what this nation has done to its Black populations from slavery forward. Indeed, as I have said before, slavery was not only devastating to Black folks physically, but I would argue that those endless hours of back-breaking free labor coupled with severe brainwashing on those plantations—believing everything White was right and everything Black was wrong—remain within us, consciously and subconsciously, emotionally and spiritually, to this very day. Through the end of slavery and legalized segregation, through the Civil Rights era, through the birth of hip-hop, right on up to Black Lives Matter. If you teach a people, any people, to hate themselves, in school, in popular culture, at church, they will develop a warped sense of what is right and what is wrong, and will go out of their way to find goodness and forgiveness even in the worst forms of oppression and injustice.

When that mindset carries on for generations, it is what Albert Einstein famously called insanity. Because we know that racism, or any other form of discrimination, is insane. Because we know it is ridiculously insane for one Black person after another, in our America, to be gunned down, simply because they are Black, because there is a paralyzing fear and blind assumption that said Black person will harm you, because you have been so contaminated with the belief that Black people are, well, monsters."

One byproduct of Christianity that was indoctrinated into enslaved

Africans is the inherent belief that a lot of Black folk still have: "No matter what, forgive White people for their actions against you." Don't believe me; look no further than the brother of Botham Jean, the man who was killed by former Dallas police Amber Guyger.

"I don't know if this is possible, but can I give her a hug, please?" Brandt Jean asked the judge, after telling Guyger that his main desire wasn't for her to go to jail but to "give your life to Christ." As the two shared a tight hug, the courtroom was largely quiet except for the sounds of sobbing. "After seeing what happened and the reason why it happened, and after seeing how people could forgive, I truly hope that people will see that it wasn't just us saying words. I know, for a fact, that it was something greater than us, using us to bring our city together." Said Chris Singleton, whose mother was assassinated in the Mother Emmanuel AME church in Charleston, South Carolina by Dylann Roof.

In no way shape, form, or fashion is it my place to tell someone who just lost their older brother, mother, or loved one how they are supposed to grieve. However, what was incredibly striking was the way that Brandt Jean chose to use his religion as the vehicle to forgiveness. He subsequently committed this act in front of the jury, who then deliberated, and although Amber Guyger could have received 90 years in prison, she was given a 10-year sentence with the possibility of parole after five years.

"Forgive us our debts as we also have forgiven our debtors. ... For if you forgive other people when they sin against you, your Heavenly Father will also forgive you." (Matthew 6:12, 14)

The criminal justice system as we know was and in many ways still is rooted in White Supremacy. This White woman, who happened to be a police officer, shot a young Black man in cold blood in his own apartment, and received a lighter sentence than some of my friends who are currently incarcerated for selling marijuana. The judge came down from behind the bench and gave her a hug. The bailiff stroked her hair with a brush. She was given a Bible and told that she was forgiven before being led out of the courtroom. Across the country, people were shocked at how the sentencing played out. Jemar Tisby described it as such.

> "Some viewed Brandt's actions as a stunning example of forgiveness, a moment of grace and tenderness that briefly bridged the chasm between races and provided an example for all to emulate. Although Christians of different backgrounds shared a variety of responses, this moment was especially celebrated by White Christians. It seems to indicate a desire to hastily move on from the wrong done and offer a perfect picture of reconciliation."

> "Perhaps, with just the right amount of compassion, some believe we can erase the color line. But when another Black man has been murdered by a person charged to "serve and protect," forgiveness should neither be demanded nor assumed.
> "But what must be understood is that when tragedies such as the murder of a Black man by a White police officer occur, they aren't just felt by one Black person. The Black community feels the impact.

But the deeper question is, just *why* do Black people so often feel compelled to forgive White people for their injustice towards us? Why do so many White people feel that Black people can endure the worst kind of atrocities and simply move on? Why do so many White people expect forgiveness, and not justice?

If White people expect all Black people to extend forgiveness as quickly as Brandt Jean did, then they understand neither Black people nor Black pain.

Black grief is a community project. It is felt widely but dealt with individually. Some go to therapy. Some participate in demonstrations. Others write op-eds. Everyone is entitled to their own process.

As Brandt stated, he speaks for himself.

What is lost in the tearful embrace between a murdered man's brother and the killer are the words of Botham's mother.

"There is much to be done by the city of Dallas," she said. "The corruption that we saw during this process must stop."

Instant absolution minimizes the magnitude of injustice. It distracts attention from the systemic change needed to prevent such tragedies from occurring.

The same Bible that urges forgiveness also urges justice.

"Learn to do right; seek justice. Defend the oppressed. Take up the cause of the fatherless; plead the case of the widow." (Isaiah 1:17).

"Black forgiveness as a response to White racism is an act of faith in God and of self-preservation. With all that Black people have endured over four centuries of racial oppression, forgiveness protects the heart from the consuming heat of hatred. It ensures that people who have been wounded don't have to constantly relive the injury. The act of forgiveness honors God, who forgives undeserving people, when someone extends it to someone else who is similarly undeserving." (Jemar Tisby, 2019 Washington Post article, "White Christians, do not cheapen the hug and message of forgiveness from Botham Jean's brother")

No one should mistake Black forgiveness, whenever and if ever it is offered, for complacency with racial injustice. No one should assume that a public act of mercy on the part of one Black person eclipses the demands for change from an entire community.

Black forgiveness is costly. It requires us to absorb wrongdoing even as we continue to work for justice. Black forgiveness becomes cheapened when we take it for granted.

Black forgiveness is admirable when it is freely given and not demanded or expected. And the best response to Black forgiveness is to prevent the harm that makes it necessary in the first place." "A lot of Black people don't want to be on the wrong side of God. It's less about wanting White people to like us or think kindly of us, and more so making sure that we are on the right side of God. Whenever we leave this Earth, God will say "Well done, my good and faithful servant." – KJ Kearney

Where did this feeling come from? I pondered this question while watching the critically acclaimed film, 12 Years a Slave. The story is based on the life of Solomon Northup, a free man from upstate New York who is an acute businessman and violinist. Solomon is tricked into coming to Washington D.C. for a performance, and subsequently sold into slavery, having his name changed to "Platt"

– a runaway from Georgia. He is initially sold to a slave master who is certain that Solomon is not like the other enslaved persons on his plantation. However, even still, even in his kindness, he keeps Solomon in bondage. Ironically, the same time that Solomon is brought, his master also purchased a woman who was a mother of three small children. The woman, Eliza, begged and pleaded to be sold with her children, but was merely slapped in the face and told to shut up. After she arrived on the plantation, the wife of the Slave owner told her "You just need some rest, your children will soon be forgotten." The next scene spoke volumes:

SOLOMON

"Stop it! Stop!"

SOLOMON

"You let yourself be overcome by sorrow. You will drown in it." **ELIZA**

"Have you stopped crying for your children? You make no sounds, but will you ever let them go in your heart?"

SOLOMON

"They are as my flesh... "

ELIZA

"Then who is distressed? Do I upset the Mistress and the Master? Do you care less for my loss than their well-being?"

SOLOMON

"Master Ford is a decent man."

ELIZA

"He is a slaver."

SOLOMON

"Under the circumstances"

ELIZA

"Under the circumstances he is a slaver! But you truckle at his boot-

- Under the circumstances he is a slaver! Christian only in his proclamations. Separated me from my precious babies for lack of a few dollars. But you truckle at his boot."

SOLOMON

"No…"

ELIZA

"You luxuriate in his favor."

SOLOMON

"I survive. I will not fall into despair. I will offer up my talents to Master Ford. I will keep myself hearty until freedom is opportune."

ELIZA

"Ford is your opportunity. Do you think he does not know that you are more than you suggest? But he does nothing for you. Nothing. You are no better than prized livestock. Call for him. Call. Tell him of your previous circumstances and see what it earns you...*Solomon*.

So, you've settled into your role as Platt, then?

SOLOMON (defensive)

"My back is thick with scars from protesting my freedom. Do not accuse me!"

ELIZA

"I accuse you of nothing. I cannot accuse. I have done many dishonorable things to survive. And for all of them I have ended up here... No better than if I had stood up for

myself. God forgive me... Forgive me. Oh, Solomon, let me weep for my children."

This scene speaks in large part to the indoctrination that Christianity and White Supremacy has had on Black people. Even when in bondage, you are taught to love your master and give him/her the benefit of the doubt. Your self-esteem is ripped away in a way that makes you place all others above yourself. This essentially brings us to a point in which we see White people as synonymous with Christianity, and if Christ was in fact perfect, then White people by default, must be inherently better than anyone else. Although this is not how the religion of Christianity is supposed to be interpreted, it is in many ways taught overtly and covertly as such. This leads to a major reason why in most instances of despair, Black people are willing to forgive White people and many White people expect forgiveness from Black people with little to no retribution. The moment in which Black people ask for accountability, they are labeled as troublemakers, "rebel rousers", or a label that describes them in a way that goes against not only the Christian values, but also their moral obligation to bring about and maintain peace.

While writing this, my emotions began to get the best of me. I cried a few times, felt angry while researching, questioned the motives of some people that were close to me, and I couldn't quite understand why. It was while reading an article written by Chauncey Devega, that I began to understand what I was feeling.

Black America owes no forgiveness: How Christianity Hinders Racial Justice

By Chauncey Devega

"On the one-year anniversary of the death of an 18-year-old Black teenager named Michael Brown by a (now confessed racist) White police officer named Darren Wilson in Ferguson, Missouri, Brown's mother, Lezley McSpadden, was asked if she forgave Darren Wilson

141

for his cruel and wanton act of legal murder. She told Al Jazeera that she will "never forgive" Darren Wilson and that "he's evil, his acts were devilish."

Her response is unusual. Its candor is refreshing. Lezley McSpadden's truth-telling reveals the full humanity and emotions of Black folks, and by doing so defies the norms which demand that when Black Americans suffer, they do so stoically, and always in such a way where forgiveness for racist violence is a given, an unearned expectation of White America.

The expectation that Black people will always and immediately forgive the violence done to them by the State, or individual White people, is a bizarre and sick American ritual.

The necropolis of Black bodies in the Age of Obama provides many examples of the ritual.

Less than a month after her son Samuel Dubose was executed by a thug cop, his mother, Audrey Dubose was asked during a press conference, if she forgave Ray Tensing. She answered "I can forgive him. I can forgive anybody. God forgave us."

After Dylann Roof massacred nine Black Americans in a Charleston, South Carolina church their families were asked to forgive the White racist terrorist.

Rituals reinforce social norms, values, and beliefs. Rituals can empower some groups and individuals; rituals can also serve to weaken and oppress others.

The ritual of immediate and expected Black forgiveness for the historic and contemporary suffering visited upon the Black community by White America reflects the complexities of the color line.

Black Americans may publicly—and this says nothing of just and righteous private anger, upset, and desire for justice and revenge— be so quick to forgive White violence and injustice because it's a tactic and strategy for coping with life in a historically White supremacist society. If Black folks publicly expressed their anger and lack of forgiveness at centuries of White transgressions they could and were beaten, raped, murdered, shot, stabbed, burned alive, run out of town, hung, put in prisons, locked up in insane asylums, fired from their jobs, their land stolen from them, and kicked out of schools. Even in the post-civil rights era and the Age of Obama, being branded with the veritable scarlet letter of being an "angry" Black man or "angry" Black woman, can result in their life opportunities being significantly reduced.

The African American church is also central to the Black American ritual of forgiveness. A belief in fantastical and mythological beings was used to fuel struggle and resistance in a long march of liberation and dignity against White Supremacy, injustice, and degradation.

The notion of "Christian forgiveness" as taught by the Black church could also be a practical means of self-medication, one designed to stave off existential malaise, and to heal oneself in the face of the quotidian struggles of life under American Apartheid.

Likewise, some used Christianity and the Black church to teach passivity and weakness in the face of White terrorism because some great reward supposedly awaits those who suffer on Earth. The public mask of public Black forgiveness and peace was also a tool that was used during the long Black Freedom Struggle as a means of demonstrating the honor, humanity, dignity, and civic virtue of Black Americans--a group who only wanted their just and paid for in blood (and free labor) civil rights.

The ritual of immediate and expected Black forgiveness fulfills the expectations of the White Gaze and the White Racial Frame. A lack of empathy from White America towards Black America is central to the ritual: if White folks could truly feel the pain of Black people (and First Nations, Hispanics and Latinos, and other people of color) in these times of meanness, cruelty, and violence, then immediate forgiveness would not be an expectation. Many White Americans actually believe that Black people are superhuman, magical, and do not feel pain. This cannot help but to somehow factor into the public ritual of Black people saying "I forgive" the violence visited upon them by White cops, paramilitaries, hate mongers, bureaucrats, and the State.

Whiteness is central here too. Whiteness imagines itself as benign, just, and innocent. Therefore, too many White people (especially those who have not acknowledged, renounced, and rejected White privilege) view White on Black racial violence as some type of ahistorical outlier, something that is not part of a pattern, a punctuation or disruption in American life, something not inherent to it, and thus not a norm of the country's social and political life.

Here, the ritual of African American forgiveness allows White America absolution and innocence without having to put in the deeds and necessary hard work for true justice, fairness, and equal democracy on both sides of the color line.

The Black forgiveness ritual's heaviest anchor is White anxiety and fear. As I wrote in an earlier piece, White America is deeply terrified, and has been since before the Founding, of Black righteous anger, and that White people in this country would be held accountable for the actions done both in their name, and for their collective benefit against Black people. This ahistorical and delusional dread (where in fact White Americans are experts in the practice of collective violence against people of color; the reverse has never been true) was summoned in the antebellum period by worries of "slave revolts". It still resonates in the 20th and 21st centuries with White racial paranoia about "ghetto" or "Black" riots, as well as the persistent bugaboo that is "Black crime".

When Black people say "we forgive" it is a salve for those White worries and fears.

The absurdity and uniqueness of Black Americans being naturally expected to immediately forgive the crimes and harm done to them by White people is highlighted precisely by how (White) America, both as an aggregate and as individuals, are not burdened with such a task.

One of the greatest privileges that comes with being "White" in America is the permission and encouragement to hold onto a sense of injustice, grievance, anger, and pain.

Consider the following.

The family of Kathryn Steinle—and whose death is the macabre subject for Donald Trump's race-baiting obsessions with "illegal" immigrants from Mexico—has not been publicly asked to forgive Francisco Sanchez, the man who killed her.

The families of the children murdered by the gun toting mass shooter Adam Lanza in Newtown, Connecticut were not publicly asked during a press conference if they forgave the killer.

The families of the 70 people wounded and 12 killed by James Holmes in a Colorado movie theater were not asked during a press conference to publicly forgive him.

And of course, the families of those killed on September 11, 2001, when agents of Al Qaeda attacked the United States, were not asked several weeks after the event if they forgave Osama bin Laden and his agents.

More than ten years after that faithful morning when the United States was attacked by Al Qaeda—and an era of national derangement and perpetual war was ushered into being—there are

145

survivors who will still not forgive those who wrought devastation onto their lives.

Some of them shared with the National Catholic Review how they continue to nurture their anger:

Mr. Haberman admitted, "That's a tough one for me. When I sit in court with these guys, can I forgive them? I have a hard time. I mean, they don't want my forgiveness. I think justice is the word."

Dorine and Martin Toyen of Avon, Conn., lost their daughter Amy, 24, in the World Trade Center. She was engaged to be married. "Her whole life was taken away from her," said Ms. Toyen. "There is no way I could ever forgive them."

Mr. Toyen concurred. "I want justice, not forgiveness," he said. "I'm still very bitter. Rage." If the accused "are found guilty, then I would have no qualms with the death penalty."

Ms. Noeth said the death penalty would be too easy. "The people that we lost suffered a lot more than that. I think they deserve as much pain as can possibly be inflicted on them."

If a reporter or other interviewer publicly asked those people who had their love ones stolen from them either on 9/11, at Newtown, or Littleton, if they forgave the monsters who hurt them so deeply, said person would (rightfully) be derided, mocked, and likely fired.

(White) Americans are not expected to forgive those who transgress them.

Black Americans who have lost their loved ones to police thuggery, violence, or other types of White on Black racial terrorism and murder should be allowed the same latitude and freedom of expression and feelings. Of course, they are not—such a right exists outside the ritual that is Black America's expected forgiveness for all the racist grievances and wrongs suffered by it.

This public ritual is a performance. It gives the White American public what they expect while concealing the true and private feelings of many Black Americans, the latter being a people who are not foolish or naïve enough to perpetually forgive, forget, and turn the other cheek when faced with perpetual abuse.

Perhaps, one day there will be a moment when a Black American who has suffered unjust loss and pain will tell the reporter who immediately asks them, "do you forgive the thug cop or racial terrorist who killed your unarmed child/ friend/ brother/ sister/ husband/ wife?" and they will reply, "Hell no! Not now, not ever, and you can go fuck yourself for asking such a question."

Devega's words were exactly what I felt. Such a moment of honesty and sharing will be a true step forward for racial justice and respect across the color line, as opposed to the charade and Kabuki-like Theater that now passes for the obligatory and weak "national conversation on race" that the American people have been repeatedly afflicted with in the post-civil rights era. This may sound harsh to some, but I am less concerned with how these words make people feel when I know that we live in a society that often monetizes Black trauma. Our pain is the entertainment and cultural flavor of the week for the masses, and because of such, I think it is worth exploring keeping our forgiveness, and working towards collective empowerment. We don't have to hate anyone else to love each other, but we do have to commit to loving ourselves and our own more than others if we truly want to see a change in our society.

Many know Charleston, South Carolina as the "Holy City". Rumor has it that it was given this name due to the variety of religions located within the city. Many believe that Charleston has been known for its religious tolerance since the 1700s. Not only does this city boast dozens of church steeples, but it's also home to plenty of historic synagogues. People from all over the world flocked to Charleston for religious freedom, so you'll find several different Protestant denominations in addition to Roman Catholic congregations here. However, this religious freedom was not for Black people, as Charleston was the city that had the greatest number of enslaved Africans come to and from while being shipped out across the country. Eventually, Black folk started their own church, Mother Emmanuel African Methodist Episcopal, out of necessity. Yes, the same church that Dylann Roof went into a Bible Study service, shot and killed nine people, and was fed Burger King after being apprehended. It was also the same place that immediately after the shooting, Blacks could be seen holding hands and praying outside of the church. This was followed by during the same week, several family members of the slain went on National Television and told Dylan Roof, "I forgive you." All while Dylan looked on with no remorse of the people he killed. The mothers, fathers, grandparents, children, and loved ones that he murdered. Why did the family members say that they forgave Dylann? The general consensus was the same amongst most of them. The same as the brother of Botham Jean, their faith in God called for them to forgive the other person.

While this is commendable, I often ponder would Black people forgive other Black people the same way that they forgive White people? Would White people forgive Black people if a Black person walked into a building and killed a mass group of White people? Did we forgive Al-Qaeda for 9/11?

When religion is broken down, the Pew Research center analyzed a wide variety of races and how they view religion. According to the Pew Research Center:

"Religion, particularly Christianity, has played an outsize role in African American history. While most Africans brought to the New World to be slaves were not Christians when they arrived, many of

148

them and their descendants embraced Christianity, finding comfort in the Biblical message of spiritual equality and deliverance. In post-Civil War America, a burgeoning Black church played a key role strengthening African American communities and in providing key support to the civil rights movement."

1. ***Roughly eight-in-ten (79%) African Americans self-identify as Christian****, as do seven-in-ten Whites and 77% of Latinos, according to Pew Research Center's 2014 Religious*

   Landscape Study. Most Black Christians and about half of all African Americans (53%) are associated with historically Black Protestant churches, according to the study. Smaller shares of African Americans identify with evangelical Protestantism (14%), Catholicism (5%), mainline Protestantism (4%) and Islam (2%).

About eight-in-ten African Americans identify as Christian

Religious identity breakdown, by race/ethnicity

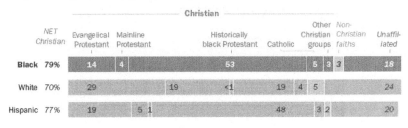

Note: Whites and blacks include only non-Hispanics. Hispanics can be of any race. "Non-Christian faiths" include Jews, Muslims, Buddhists, Hindus, other world religions and other faiths. "Other Christian groups" include Jehovah's Witnesses, Mormons, Orthodox Christians and members of other smaller Christian groups. Don't know/refused reponses not shown. Figures may not add to subtotals indicated due to rounding.
Source: 2014 U.S. Religious Landscape Study, conducted June 4-Sept. 30, 2014

PEW RESEARCH CENTER

2. *The first predominantly Black denominations in the U.S. were founded in the late 18th century, some by free Black people.*

   *Today, **the largest historically Black church in the U.S. is the National Baptist Convention U.S.A. Inc.** Other large historically Black churches include the Church of God in Christ, the African Methodist Episcopal Church (AME), and two other Baptist churches – the National Baptist Convention of America and the Progressive*

National Baptist Association Inc.

By many measures, African Americans are more religious than whites and Latinos

% of ____ who ...

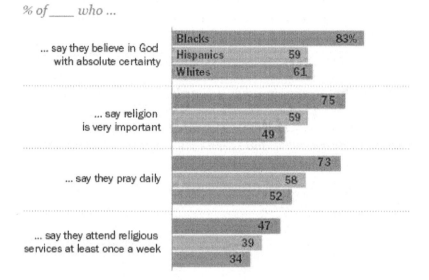

... say they believe in God with absolute certainty	Blacks 83% / Hispanics 59 / Whites 61
... say religion is very important	75 / 59 / 49
... say they pray daily	73 / 58 / 52
... say they attend religious services at least once a week	47 / 39 / 34

Note: Whites and blacks include only non-Hispanics. Hispanics can be of any race.
Source: 2014 U.S. Religious Landscape Study, conducted June 4-Sept. 30, 2014

PEW RESEARCH CENTER

3. African Americans are more religious than Whites and Latinos by many measures of religious commitment. For instance, three-quarters of Black Americans say religion is very important in their lives, compared with smaller shares of Whites (49%) and Hispanics (59%); African Americans also are more likely to attend services at least once a week and to pray regularly. Black Americans (83%) are more likely to say they believe in God with absolute certainty than Whites (61%) and Latinos (59%).

4. The share of African Americans who identify as religiously unaffiliated has increased in recent years, *mirroring national trends. In 2007, when the first Religious Landscape Study was conducted, only 12% of Black Americans said they were religiously unaffiliated — that is, atheist, agnostic or "nothing in particular." By the time the 2014 Landscape Study was conducted, that number had grown to 18%. As with the general population, younger African American adults are more likely than older African Americans to be unaffiliated. Three-in-ten (29%) African Americans between the ages of 18 and 29 say they are unaffiliated compared with only 7% of Black adults 65 and older who say this.*

5. Older African Americans are more likely than younger Black adults to be associated with historically Black Protestant churches. *While 63% of the Silent Generation (born between 1928 and 1945) say they identify with historically Black denominations, only 41% of Black Millennials say the same. (When the survey was conducted in 2014, Millennials included those born between 1981 and 1996.)*

As my good friend Mr. KJ Kearney previously stated, "A lot of Black people don't want to be on the wrong side of God. It's less about wanting White people to like us or think kindly of us, and more so making sure that we are on the right side of God. Whenever we leave this Earth, God will say "Well done, my good and faithful servant."

<u>The opposite of White Supremacy is not Racial Revenge.</u>

As it pertains to Christianity, the way to remedy the wrongs of those before us who used the religion as a weapon of oppression is not to seek revenge. In fact, for the treacherous White people who used Christianity as a method to suppress, or a vehicle to drive down a road of malice, their fate must be determined by the creator. However the system in which they created that is still prevalent today, can be addressed.

How you ask? We must be patient with people and impatient with progress. We must address the systemic inequities at a feverish pace, while being cognizant that individuals as a whole move at their own speed. The task is incredibly difficult. The task will make us want to quit on several different occasions, but we are fighting for more than just ourselves.

The gift of grace and forgiveness is a powerful tool in the battle against White Supremacy. The leverage that comes with forgiveness is even more powerful. I think distinctly to the year 2018, and I am sitting in a courtroom with a White supremacist who was on trial for a young man who at the time was 20 years old. He was an admitted White supremacist who believed that White people were better than everyone else. He came to Charlottesville, Virginia in August of 2017 because he wanted to join in with friends in "beating up some Niggers and Jews". Why I was subpoenaed by his defense attorney to testify in his trial was an absolute mystery to me. For weeks leading up to me having to go and testify, I was perplexed as to why they wanted me to come. They knew where I stood in regard to the statues, to how I felt about White Supremacy, and I was probably one of the "Niggers" that this young man wanted to come and beat up while in Virginia.

I entered the courtroom and noticed that there were not a lot of people present. There were three people on the right side of the courtroom, who I assumed was this young man's parents. Dressed in jeans and a NASCAR jacket, they scowled at me with utter disgust as I approached the bench to take my oath before testifying. The questions from his attorney were mundane at best. Questions about plans for the Unite the Right rally, questions about why I felt the statues should be moved, more questions about logistics for the actual day of the rally, and where I was personally. I honestly thought that they were wasting my time.

That was until I looked to my left and looked into the eyes of a 20-year-old who clearly was terrified. At the time I had been a high school teacher for seven years and was currently serving as a Dean of Students at an Alternative High School for troubled young people. I knew exactly what a kid who was afraid looked like. What I saw in this young man's face was more than fear. It was a realization that he had really messed up. He came to the realization that the stuff that he was learning while watching YouTube videos about the next race war was wrong. He came to the realization that he got himself involved with people who had an ideology that he didn't necessarily subscribe to. He really didn't want to hurt anyone; he was still trying to find himself. This young man, 20 years old, had been having a hard time in jail, and was soon to be sent off to prison, all because he was manipulated by older folks and indoctrinated with hate. At 20 years old, science tells us that the male frontal lobes are yet to be developed. Now, this kid was about to go to jail for making an irrational decision like most 20 year olds do. I saw myself in this young man.

When I was 20 years old, I was in college, I was finding myself, I was a leader, but I also followed my older cousins and got into a lot of really close calls with the law. I thought I knew everything about everything. I could be the perfect young man who went to church with his uncle in Manning, South Carolina on Sundays, or I could be Kaine from Menace II Society. It's been documented that during this time my friends and I said the most raunchy, homophobic, prejudice, sexist, and ignorant things that one could say on Twitter. I was finding myself. I was growing up. Over the course of time, I learned to mature. I gained new experiences. I met new people. I learned different things. All of my experiences made me a better person. The thing is, I was afforded the opportunity to become a better person while being free. This was something that the young man in the courtroom knew would not be his reality.

As my questioning was over, and I was permitted to leave, I walked over to him, bent over in his ear, and told him to keep his head up. God loves him and will see him through this. Rely on God and grow from this. You are not defined by your worst day.

I was met by his parents and reporters afterwards who both

wanted to know what I said to him? After telling them the truth, I saw the eyes of the mother change. She thanked me, gave me a hug, and went on about her business. A reporter asked me why did I do that? The answer was simple. God has granted me grace on multiple occasions. My community has granted me grace on multiple occasions. My wife has granted me grace on multiple occasions. My God has granted me grace and mercy on a daily basis. In a time like this for him, who am I not to show the same?

The pivot from grace is equity. Many people remember the fallout from the photograph of two men, one dressed in KKK garb and the other in complete Blackface, on the medical school yearbook page of Virginia Governor Ralph Northam, which surfaced in February of 2019. The picture was incredibly painful to Virginians, and his press conference addressing the matter was almost as painful and cringe worthy as the picture itself. Personally, it hurt because I knew Governor Northam personally. He and I had gone to church together, fellowshipped together, spoke on a regular basis, and I vouched for him to several of my friends during his campaign for governor. People I knew personally and had deep friendships with worked in his cabinet. How could this happen? How could he do this to us? Was he lying to us the entire time? Was he tricking us? What was going on?

I, along with several others called on Gov. Northam to resign immediately, but he made it clear that he was not going to do so. He said that resigning would be taking the easy way out. He wanted to face this issue head on. He wanted to hear from people directly how his actions hurt them. He wanted to learn about why his actions were so hurtful and understand the true history of race in our state. He wanted to embark on a journey of leading Virginia down a road of equity. He and I had very frank and candid conversations afterwards. There were many expectations placed on his office about policy measures and budget allocations to show the Commonwealth of Virginia that he meant what he said. To his credit, he's delivered on every promise made, including placing over $250 million into the state's budget for the two-state funded

HBCUs.

He proposed the following equity measures in his proposed biennial budget:

<u>Education</u>

$94.8 million over the biennium to transform Virginia's early childhood education system and increase access to at-risk three and four year olds across the Commonwealth.

$140.4 million to increase the At-Risk Add-On and better support high-needs students in grades K-12. This is the largest proposed single increase to this program in Virginia's history.

$10.6 million for school breakfast and lunch programs across the Commonwealth, to help ensure all students are healthy and prepared to learn.

Over $31 million in operating funds and over $262 million in capital funding for Virginia State University and Norfolk State University, Virginia's only public HBCUs. This is the largest proposed infusion of operating funds for Virginia public HBCUs in decades.

$145 million for the Governor's "Get Skilled, Get a Job, Give Back" program, to provide tuition-free community college to middle and low-income students in high demand fields.

$500,000 to Old Dominion University to support Virginia Symphony Orchestra minority fellowships.

<u>Housing, Healthcare, and Nutrition</u>

$92 million in new funding to address homelessness, expand the supply of affordable housing, reduce eviction rates, and provide permanent supportive housing for populations with special needs.

Nearly $22 million over the biennium to combat maternal and infant mortality and reduce the racial disparity in Virginia's maternal mortality rate.

Funding for the Virginia Department of Health to expand the Office of Health Equity, provide adult sickle cell services, and fund staff in four high-need health districts for community health pilot programs.

$3 million in non-general funding to the Federation of Virginia Food Banks, to provide child nutrition programs and increase food security across Virginia.

$7.77 million in general funding and $5.05 million in non-general funding to create a summer food security program through TANF.

Environment

$2.7 million to the Department of Environmental Quality, to be directed specifically towards environmental justice and community outreach efforts.

Criminal Justice Reform

$5.6 million for additional district court clerk positions, to ensure a more accessible, efficient, and responsive criminal justice system.

$14.8 million to establish a new public defender's office in Prince William County, and fund additional public defenders.

$6.6 million for alternative incarceration and re-entry services by expanding pretrial, local probation, and supporting pre-release and post-incarceration services.

Economic Opportunity

$1.4 million to establish and support a statewide unit to strategically source small, woman, and minority-owned (SWaM) business participation on large dollar Commonwealth contracts.

African American History/ Historical Equity

$2.5 million to support K-12 student attendance at the Black History Museum and Cultural Center of Virginia, as well as to support traveling exhibits from the center to K-12 schools.

$2 million to provide students from across the Commonwealth the ability to visit the American Civil War Museum, to better tell the truth about the Civil War and Virginia's role in it.

$300,000 to digitize, expand, and increase access to Virginia's historical highway marker program.

Over $7 million to support historic African American sites, including Freedom House, Monticello, Montpelier, and Maymont.

$1 million to support the Slavery and Freedom Heritage site in Richmond.

Budget creates an African American Cemeteries fund.

Government

$1.2 million to fully fund the Office of Diversity, Equity, and Inclusion.

Funding to pay Governor's fellows and interns with the Office of the Governor.

Governor Northam is like many White people that I have encountered. Governor Northam is like many Black people that I have encountered. Governor Northam, like all of us, is a work in progress. To bring forth tangible change, White people and Black people will have to work together at a grassroots level, at a policy level, and at a spiritual level. People from across the racial spectrum will have to band together to demand changes in policy and resource reallocation. Organizations and elected officials alike will have to take bold steps to carry out those plans. People as a whole will have to continue rallying together to push for change.

Does this mean that Black people have to forgive every treacherous act committed against us? Does this mean that White people have to beg for forgiveness at the feet of every Black person that they meet for the rest of their lives? Does this mean that Black people have to always take the high road? Does this mean that White people will immediately understand the harm that they have caused, and stop doing harmful things? Does this mean that Black people are allowed to seek revenge or vengeance against those who have caused us pain? Does this mean that every White person will take to the streets and fight on the behalf of every social justice issue that comes along? The answer, in my opinion, is two-fold. If we want to heal our land, we have to heal ourselves. If we want a better society, as individuals, we have to commit to being better people. With better people, comes better actions. With better actions, comes tangible results that have long term effects. If we want to destroy our land, then we can do unto others as they have always done to us. The choice is up to every individual person, but I hope that we all choose the option that leaves a land for my daughters and future grandchildren to play in. I hope we choose the option that allows my grandchildren the ability to work with others and accomplish the community that Dr. King, Brother Malcolm, Rabbi Sarah, Sister Jane Elliot, Priest William, and even the Pope dreamt about.

10. BLACK PRIVILIGE AND WHITE POWER

Black Lives Won't Matter Until Black Politics Do

I realize, even as a Black man, I have privilege. I am well aware that even as a Black man living in the former capital of the Confederacy, the Commonwealth of Virginia, I still have a great deal of privilege. I'm pretty good friends with both the current and former governor of our state. I have access to several U.S. Senators and Congresspersons. I have access to state and local representatives from across the country. I have access to people with resources. I have the ability to live a life and provide for my family in a way that I am happy with, and when I look in the mirror, I am well aware that I have more work to do in relation to my own growth, but I have access to a lot.

One of the things that changed my life was winning my city council election and becoming the vice-mayor of the City of Charlottesville at the age of 29.

I live in one of the last predominately Black neighborhoods in my city. My neighbors are very protective of my family and me. The community as a whole usually tries to look out for my wife and daughters. I acknowledge that this is not the norm for most Black folk. While that privilege remains true, the unfortunate part is that it is necessary because we have people come and throw rocks at our house, drive by and yell obscenities, and try and use other tactics to intimidate us. I have a doctoral degree, served on the State Board of Education, and I am the youngest person to be a department chairman at my institution. These positions and titles have allowed my family – in some ways, to not have the same strains as others who look like me, but even with these titles, I am regularly called Dr. Nigger on social media. I am an avid runner, and when I am running throughout my community and neighborhood it feels good to see someone throw up a fist, say "Keep going, Wes", or "We appreciate you" all in love. However, there have been countless times when I have been jogging and called a Nigger, told "You ruined my city", or received another obscenity. Personally, I believe this shows how even when some black people reach levels of privilege, they are still forced to deal with the byproducts of white supremacy. There is no relief or reprieve from white supremacy when you are Black. It's a consistent cloud of knowing that you have to play and abide by a different set of rules. If you speak out, you become a target. If you are quiet you still could be affected by it, and in your silence, you are essentially saying that the systems that are in place are ok. It's a conundrum that we have to be willing to face and fight back against.

I firmly believe that Black lives as a whole will not matter to the masses until the policies that specifically pertain to the advancement of Black people begin to matter. Access and privilege are one thing, but what happens when you don't have it? We have heard about health disparities and how they affect African Americans in regard to their White counterparts, but the data only tells one part of the story. In April of 2020, our country was being ravished by a deadly disease known as COVID19. While many will be able to look back at this tumultuous time and analyze the economic impact, the fact that African Americans were killed at much higher rates than any other subgroup, or the overall incompetency of our President at the time to see how damaging this disease was to our nation, what will always remain in my mind is privilege and access. In March of 2020, I received a phone call from a gentleman who I have the utmost respect for, Mr. Gil Bland.

Mr. Bland was the chairman of the Hampton Roads Urban League, an astute businessman, a philanthropist, a community leader, and a civil servant. In addition to these titles, Mr. Bland was the chairman of the newly formed Commonwealth of Virginia African American Advisory Board. This board of appointees from across the state was the first of its kind and was a very big deal for our state for a myriad of reasons. There were only 20 people selected, and I was fortunate to be appointed to the board. This is significant, because Mr. Bland and I began to develop a relationship and often discussed different ways to help our community. In addition to serving as the chairman of the African American Advisory Board, he also serves as the chairman of the board for Sentara Hospital. Serving as chairman, Mr. Bland was pushing the hospital to make more of a concerted effort when it came to the testing of African Americans for COVID19. While Sentara was looking to implement testing on some scale across the state, I received the aforementioned call about offering similar testing in Charlottesville. I accepted, and subsequently had a phone call with my mayor, Madame Nikiyah Walker, our city manager, a couple of pastors, and representatives from the hospital. This subsequently led to a larger community group and over the next few weeks we began to offer hundreds of COVID19 tests with wrap around services for those who tested positive to members of low income, public housing, and other at-risk communities within the city and area. We were later joined by the University of Virginia Hospital system, and as community and health providers, began to provide weekly testing for communities of color and those who needed testing. It felt good, and I was incredibly proud to have played a role in helping the community, but something ate at me every night when I went to sleep. *What about the communities that didn't have someone as connected living in their city? Who helps them?*

My father, who lives in Little River, South Carolina, had a stroke in the spring of 2020, and because of his condition, I made a commitment to help out with the family as much as I could. It was roughly a five-hour drive from Charlottesville to Little River, but I was determined to make the trek down the interstate at least twice a month. While making the drive, my wife made me promise to wear gloves, my mask, frequently use hand sanitizer, and wash my hands at all times. While traveling, one of my favorite things to do was stop in small rural Black towns along the way and look at the community. As a former city councilman, I enjoyed looking at the infrastructure of the city, the resources, if any, that were available, and more than anything else, the population. One thing became painfully obvious. From rural Virginia, to rural North Carolina, to rural South Carolina, very few people wore masks and there was little to no COVID19 testing. I made an assumption about some of the health conditions of the people who I met, spoke with through my mask, and saw while looking out of my window, and it wasn't good. *Who helps them?* Where is the connected person that sits on the governor's board that can help bring in hundreds of tests? Where are the people who can rally resources for these communities? What all of this made me feel was a harsh reality. Yes, I as one individual have a great deal of access and privilege. In many cases, my privilege turns out to help my family, my community, and my city as a whole. However, what about everyone else? Who helps them?

Some may ask, what is this Black Privilege that I speak of? How can Black privilege even exist in a society that is predicated on White Supremacy? Well…to a certain extent, I would argue that there has always been Black Privilege since the time that the White masters wanted to begin playing psychological games on enslaved Africans. Privilege, are some people who live on the plantation being forced to work in the field, be subjected to the elements, while others are permitted to remain in the house, while "being told" that they are somewhat better than others because they don't have to be subjected to the same conditions as their counterparts. However, here is the part some, *not all,* of the enslaved back then understood, and *others* didn't. Just because the "massa" allows you to drink lemonade and sleep in the Big house, doesn't make you immune to the harsh realities of the system of slavery. This same lesson applies to many African Americans who have achieved higher levels of social status than others. This is the same lesson that I have been wrestling with and trying to figure out exactly what to do with it. White Supremacy is, as my good friend Quinton Harrell would say, *illmatic*. Some African Americans have made more money than others due to entertainment, athletics, or they are in a particular industry that allows them to "believe" that they are immune to systemic oppression. Some of us have achieved a certain political status that allows us to be invited to a variety of different events. Many of us have come to believe that we are somewhat better than others, because of these things. Our privilege and our access has made many of us comfortable, which subsequently leads to many of us having a false sense of entitlement. Many of us have a false sense of security, and a belief that because we as individuals are ok, that our society as a whole is making tremendous strides and those who are not in our position are not there because of their own doing. It is important for society, both Black and White people, to recognize the fact that your status, your income, your followers on social media, or anything else that we seem to think makes us immune to White Supremacy is a fallacy. It is a facade. It is not true. LeBron James has had the word Nigger spray painted on his house. Dr. Henry Gates, the esteemed professor from Harvard, has been arrested and detained outside of his own house because law enforcement thought that he was trying to break in. Even President Barack Obama had to produce his birth certificate, while sitting as President of the country, to quell rumors and chatter from White supremacists and their counterparts about whether or not he is truly American. Not only are Black people not immune to these kinds of acts of bigotry, but for many Black people, they are so far removed from any privilege or access, the systems that have been put in place will literally rip apart their families, prohibit their advancement, and in some instances, kill them. How do we fix it?

First, we have to admit that these systems exist, and work to improve the inequities in a tangible way. Please understand that when I say we, I mean we as a human race, but specifically, I mean White people.

Second, we have to commit ourselves to understanding that if I have access and resources, then my brother or sister has access and resources. This is for both Black people and White people. When I speak to Black people and I tell them that I have no fear of my brother or sister, they often look at me like I am crazy. I am not super-negro or anything, but I have jogged down the blocks of the "wild 100s" in Chicago, walked the streets of Brownsville Brooklyn, hung out in Compton, California, and sat and broke bread in some of the most "dangerous" places in America according to the narrative that is often perpetuated by the media and the like. I say those things to point out that our people are not to be afraid of, yet our people are to be loved. The notion that we have to hate each other is a fallacy that has existed even prior to the first group of enslaved Africans being stolen and brought over centuries ago. The small subtleties of loving each other include buying from Black owned businesses and giving each other the benefit of the doubt when someone makes a mistake. It means not running to trash your brother or sister online when you have an unfortunate incident at one of their businesses. I often think about how many of us have frequented McDonalds for decades. We have had our order wrong, had bad service, or just an unfortunate experience on several occasions. The difference is, we still continue to give McDonalds our money. We have to show the same kind of grace with our own. I am not saying to be foolish nor I am not saying to make excuses, I am saying to show grace. If we build our economic power, we can build our political power. Think about it. Who is more willing to help the young sister or brother who is a senior in high school a few dollars short to go off to college, the neighborhood McDonalds or the mom and pop grocery store/restaurant that's been in the community for years? By that same notion, those of us with resources or with businesses must commit ourselves to providing high quality and high service to all people, and specifically our people. Some things are challenging, but we accomplish so much more together, than we do divided.

Third, we have to deprogram ourselves from the White Supremacy that has indoctrinated our way of thinking. Honestly, ask yourself, do you think that White people could survive the atrocities that Black people have had to, and then tell themselves to pull themselves up by their bootstraps? I think not. However, this doesn't mean that all skin folk are kinfolk, nor does it mean all White people are here to hurt or harm us. The deprogramming is for all of us, every race. We have to commit ourselves to understanding the systems at play and doing the difficult work of challenging said systems to change. It's not by mistake that most of the AP classes in most high schools are majority White, and most of the special education classes are majority Black. It's not by mistake that African Americans represent nearly 13% of the student population, yet only 1.8% of all teachers are Black males. It's not by mistake that African Americans represent nearly 13% of the population in the country, but nearly half of all of the inmates in prison. These systems have been in play, and until we are willing to commit ourselves to undoing them, they will remain in play. How do we undo them? Malcolm X said it best, with the ballot. The ballot is not just about voting, it's not just about running for office. The ballot is *"owning"* our politics, and centering the needs of our people first. The ballot is a multipronged approach that enables us to be able to put a major dent into the atrocities that have happened to our people. Here is a quick breakdown in the most simplistic way that I can think of:

Scenario 1

1) When you register to vote, you become a part of the political process.
2) When you are registered to vote, you are eligible to serve on juries.
3) When you are eligible to serve on a jury, you could be selected to serve when a police officer shoots an unarmed Black person.
4) If you are on the jury, you proceed, without bias, but with fairness, accountability, and subsequently justice is more likely to be served.

Scenario 2

1) When you register to vote, you become a part of the political process.

2) As a registered voter, you are allowed to run for political office.

3) When you run and win a seat on your local school board or city council, you are able to write, adopt, or amend the policies that have an effect on your community.

    a. If your schools aren't teaching about Black history, don't use textbooks that highlight the value or importance of Black history, you can advocate to change it. If your schools have poor policies that prohibit the advancement of Black children into higher-level classes while having several policies that advocate for Black children to be placed into special education, you as a school board member can advocate to change that.

    b. If the municipality where you live is putting little to no resources into the communities that have a majority Black population (i.e. poor road infrastructure, food deserts, lack of after school activities or programs for young people, issues with affordable housing, over-policing, etc....) the body that has a direct impact on those items and more, is the city council. The city council also creates and appoints members to local boards and commissions who often provide the recommendations to the city council about changes to the community.

There are countless reasons why we should be involved in the political process, why we have to do more than advocate online or outside, but all of it comes down to us being involved. Yes, we have every reason to not trust the system in place. We have every reason to not want to be involved. We have every reason to feel defeated, but that, to a certain extent is the easy way out. If you want to disappoint the ancestors who literally died for us to have the right to engage in the same civil liberties that were denied to them, then be my guest. However, I am also a firm believer that if you aren't willing to put in the work to create the change, you can't complain about the progress or lack thereof.

When it comes to progress, I am no longer one who believes that just because we are Black, we have to be beholden to the Democratic Party or the Republican Party while they take our votes for granted. The days in which we trade our votes for nothing in return have to end. Sean "P. Diddy" Combs and I were having a conversation and he was adamant that our vote has to be transactional. Initially, I thought that he was confused, and thought there is no way that this will ever happen. However, he is right. When we look at the provisions and resource allocations that the Federal government has made for Asian-Americans, Native Americans, and several other constituency groups, the main group that has suffered the most have been Black people. The group that has received the least, also Black people. Until we begin to develop our own political structures, things will be that much more challenging for us.

We are often told that education is the greatest equalizer. We are often told that if we vote, then we can make the changes to our communities that we want to see. Making good grades, getting the necessary credentials and degrees to look good on paper, and being politically astute are important for sure, but the fact remains that you are still Black in America. In America, a society that is rooted and based in capitalism, what we respect the most is economics. We must develop policy around increasing the capital of Black people in America. Many remember the "I Have a Dream" speech by Dr. Martin Luther King Jr., and his call for equality. While yes, it was a rallying cry for equality, its original intent was to call for an end to economic inequality for all people and to demand the right to gainful employment for all.

"In a sense we've come to our nation's capital to cash a check. When the architects of our Republic wrote the magnificent words

167

of the Constitution and the Declaration of Independence, they were
signing a promissory note to which every American was to fall heir
... Instead of honoring this sacred obligation, America has given
  the
Negro people a bad check, a check which has come back marked
'insufficient funds.' But we refuse to believe that the bank of justice
is bankrupt."

Dr. King was as right then as he is today. There is a false assumption throughout the nation that lies amongst many. The false assumption that people who work the hardest can move up the proverbial ladder for prosperity is a fallacy. One cannot lift themselves up by the bootstrap if they don't have any boots. In order to get the boots, there has to be a two-prong approach. There has to be a commitment from our society, our municipalities, our state and local governments, and our federal government to be intentional about leveling the playing field, specifically for Black people. We have seen the Federal government make specific monetary allocations for Japanese Americans, we have seen the Federal government print off $2 Trillion to address the needs of the country during the COVID19 epidemic, and we have seen laws, policies, and resources passed, adopted, and allocated in ways in which we have never seen before. Why can't the same be done for Black people?

In my opinion, these efforts have to be advocated for, adopted, and allocated on a state and local level. When we look at African American business development, contract spending, specific allocations for economic empowerment via resources for home ownership, educational achievement, and equitable resource distribution are more achievable and attainable on a state and local level. Why? Because local and state government have fewer resources, but more autonomy over what to do directly with the resources that they have. Yes, education will improve our lives. Voting will put the people in place to address the needs of a people who have been historically mistreated, but economic equity will allow for us to have the resources to be able to provide for and sustain ourselves. I am not asking the government to give me a pair of boots, I am simply asking that they remove the barriers on the trail that will puncture, cut, and scrape my feet if I don't have boots on.

Lastly, be patient with people, and impatient with progress. If this was easy, it would've already been done.

We Need White Allies *and* White Accomplices

One of the statements that I think every White person who is looking to use their privilege has said is "I want to get involved, but I don't know where to start." The statement itself is often one that can lead to paralysis. I think it is important for every White person to decide if they want to be an ally, an accomplice, or a bystander? The distinctions are clear in my eyes.

An ally is an individual who uses their privilege and power to advocate and speak on behalf of someone else who does not hold the same privilege. Allyship means more than just becoming aware of an issue, it means that you will also take action in anyway that brings about an end to the injustice. An ally isn't defined by simply believing in the need for change. An ally is defined by what actions they take in regard to bringing about change.

An accomplice in the fight to dismantle White Supremacy in a social justice context, speaks to a sense of community which derives from the Latin term *complicare,* which means "folding together." An ally will, for the most part, engage in activism by working with or standing with individuals and/or groups from a marginalized community. An accomplice on the other hand, will focus on working with organizations and entities that are focused on dismantling the very structures that uphold White Supremacy.

Marginalized communities as a whole need both, allies and accomplices, but only you as an individual can determine which you will be. At the very minimum, every White person must choose one. Unfortunately, too many have chosen to be bystander.

A *bystander* turns their head the other way when they see a racist act against someone, in both public and private. A bystander will say that they don't want to get involved, it's none of their business, and by doing so, condone the racist attacks. Yes, by not speaking up, you are condoning.

I don't want to get into a long diatribe about what one can do and not do. Instead, I would like for you to hear it directly from a fellow White person.

Sister Corinne Shutack came up with the most comprehensive list that I have ever seen for White people. She originally titled it, "65 Things White People Can Do for Racial Justice." I pulled out several that I firmly stand behind.

1. *Google whether your local police department currently outfits all on-duty police officers with a body-worn camera and requires that the body-worn camera be turned on immediately when officers respond to a police call. If they don't, write to your city or town government representative and police chief to advocate for it. The racial make-up of your town doesn't matter*
    — This needs to be standard everywhere. Multiply your voice by soliciting others to advocate as well, writing on social media about it, writing op-eds, etc.

2. *Google whether your city or town currently employs evidence-based police de-escalation trainings. The racial make-up of your town doesn't matter — This needs to be standard everywhere. Write to your city or town government representative and police chief and advocate for it. Multiply your voice by soliciting others to advocate as well, writing on social media about it, writing op-eds, etc.*

3. *More and more stories of Black folks encountering racism are being documented and shared through social media — whether it's at a hotel, with the police, in a coffee shop, at a school, etc. When you see such a post, call the organization, company, or*

170

institution involved to tell them how upset you are. Then share the post along with the institution's contact information, spreading the word about what happened and encouraging others to contact the institution as well. Whether the company initiated the event or failed to protect a POC during an onslaught by a third party, they need to hear from us.

4. *If you or a friend is an educator, buy said friend books that feature POC as protagonists and heroes, no matter the racial make-up of the class, and/or purchase educational toys that feature POC, such as finger puppets, Black History Flashcards, etc. for their classroom. Use these items year-round, not just in February. The racial make-up of students doesn't matter — kids of every race need to know American history and be exposed to people from different races, religions, and countries. If the friend is interested, buy them for your pal's classroom. Don't be shy to ask Facebook friends that you haven't actually talked to in ten years.*

5. *Work on ensuring that Black educators are hired where Black children are being taught. If you want to know more about why and how this makes a difference for Black children, check out Malcolm Gladwell's podcast about race and education. There are some really good nuggets in there about how schools can support the achievement of Black students — from ensuring Black students aren't closed out of gifted programs by using test results instead of White teachers' recommendations to the influence that having a Black teacher has on a Black student's education to the importance to fostering a school ethos wherein Black students think, "This school is here for me."*

6. *Many companies have recruiting channels that are predominantly White. Work with your HR department to recruit Americans who are descendants of slaves. Recruiting from HBCUs is a good start. Work to put descendants of slaves already hired under supportive managers.*

7. *Donate to anti-White Supremacy work such as your local Black Lives Matter Chapter, the National Council for Incarcerated and Formerly Incarcerated Women, the NAACP, Southern Poverty Law Center, United Negro College Fund, Black Youth Project 100, Color of Change, The Sentencing Project, Families against Mandatory Minimums, A New Way of Life, and Dream Defenders. Join some of these list-serves and take action as their emails dictate.*

8. *Support Black businesses. Find them on WeBuyBlack, The Black Wallet, and Official Black Wall Street.*

9. *Bank Black. It doesn't have to be all of your checking or savings. Opening up an account with some money is better than no account at all. Google Black owned banks to find a bank.*

10. *Don't buy from companies that use prison labor.*

11. *Find and join a local "White space" to learn more about and talk out the conscious and unconscious biases us White folks have. If there's not a group in your area, start one.*

12. *Buy books, choose TV shows and movies, and opt for toys for your kids, nieces, nephews, etc that show people from different races, religions, countries and that teach real American history. A few ideas: the books, toys, and flashcards from #4.*

13. *Decolonize your bookshelf.*

14. *Listen without ego and defensiveness to people of color. Truly listen. Don't scroll past articles written by people of color — Read them.*

15. *Don't be silent about that racist joke. Silence is support.*

16. *Find out how slavery, the Civil War, and the Jim Crow era are being taught in your local school. Is the school teaching about post-Civil War convict leasing, the parent to our current mass*

incarceration system? Talking about slavery alone, is your school showing images such as Gordon's scourged back, a slave ship hold, and a slave nurse holding her young master? Are explorers, scientists, politicians, etc... who are POC discussed? Are male and female authors who are POC on the reading lists? Are Japanese internment camps being discussed? There are a lot of great resources out there with a little googling, like PBS's resources for teaching slavery, Teaching for Change, and The National Association for Multicultural Education.

17. *Seek out a diverse group of friends for your kids.*

18. *Seek out a diverse group of friends for you. Practice real friendship and intimacy by listening when POC talk about their experiences and their perspectives. They're speaking about their pain.*

19. *Call or write to your national legislators, state legislators, and governor in favor of affirmative action. Encourage friends to do the same.*

20. *Write to your college/university about implementing diversity strategies that effectively promote racial, ethnic, and socioeconomic diversity on campus. Write to the public universities your taxpayer dollars support about implementing these diversity strategies.*

21. *Recognize that in the same way saying "slavery is a necessary evil" (Thomas Jefferson's words) was acceptable by many in 1820, the same way saying "separate but equal" was acceptable by many in 1940, choosing to not condemn White nationalism, the fact that Black people are 2.7 times as likely to be killed by police than White people, the fact that unarmed Black Americans are roughly five times as likely as unarmed White Americans to be shot and killed by a police officer, that the fact the Black imprisonment rate for drug offenses is about*

5.8 times higher than it is for Whites, etc are acts of overt racism in 2019.

22. *Donate to groups that are working to put women of color into elected office, to get out the vote, and to restore voting rights to disenfranchised voters.*

23. *Check out Black movies, TV, and other media that show POC as lead characters and in their full humanity. Queen Sugar, Insecure, Dear White People, The Carmichael Show, Blackish, Grownish, Atlanta, 2 Dope Queens, Black Panther, A Wrinkle in Time, Get Out, Girls Trip, Mudbound, How to Get Away with Murder, Scandal, The Cloverfield Paradox, Sorry to Bother You, Blindspotting, BlackkKlansman, Little, If Beale Street Could Talk, and Queen and Slim are a few. Share them with friends.*

24. *When people say that Black Lives Matter is a violent/terrorist group, explain to them that there are fringe groups that are being misrepresented as part of BLM. If conservatives don't want to be lumped in with the KKK, they can't lump violent protesters in with BLM.*

25. *Be honest about our history. One genocide, another genocide, then apartheid. It sucks, but it's true. We'll never be free from our history unless we're honest about it. Denial is our pathology, but the truth will set us free.*

26. *Talk to the White people you know who aren't clearly upset by White Supremacy. Use "I" statements and "I care" messages ("I feel [feeling] when you [behavior]"). They need to know you see a problem. Call them out, and call them in. As a start, ask them to watch the videos in #23. For people you know who've been radicalized by FOX News and other nationalist (not conservative) media, who've been so pummeled with fear and hatred of "the other" that they've become ISIS-like towards others, how can you and other family and friends guide them*

through conversation to show them that their actions are now in direct contrast with the values they feign to purport?

27. *Don't become the monster, as you try to kill the monster. As Gloria Steinem says, "The ends don't justify the means. The means are the ends."*

28. *Credit Black men and women.*

11 SO NOW WHAT? NEXT STEPS FOR A MORE PERFECT UNION

I live in Charlottesville, Virginia. An area where you cannot drive five miles without being reminded that this was, and in the eyes of some still is, the home of Thomas Jefferson. About forty-five minutes away from the city that I love is a place known as Orange County, the home of James Madison, also known as the man who is considered by many to be the author of the United States Constitution. Both of these men owned slaves. Both of these men have written about what they believed to be their internal confliction with owning other human beings. Both had the opportunity to free their slaves. For all of their high praise and accolades, neither of the two did.

The Preamble to the U.S. Constitution reads as such:

"We the people of the United States, in order to form a more perfect union, establish justice, insure domestic tranquility, provide for the common defense, promote the general welfare, and secure the blessings of liberty to ourselves and our posterity, do ordain and establish this Constitution for the United States of American."

The Preamble outlines six main goals.

1. Form a more perfect union: to help keep the country together as one

2. Establish justice: provide laws and punishments in a fair manner

3. Ensure domestic tranquility: keep peace within the country

4. Provide for the common defense: protect the citizens (military)

5. Promote the general welfare: look out for the general well-being of all citizens

6. Secure the blessings for liberty: protect freedom now and for the future

The Constitution, the Preamble, the thought that all "men" were created equal, was nonsense then as much as it is now. To some, this document is one that every American should believe in, pledge their allegiance to, and uphold with the utmost level of honor. To others, the words on the document are no more than words on a piece of paper that never have been for them. So, when asking Black people to "Pledge allegiance to the flag" in grade school, middle school, or thereafter, think about what you are really asking. When asking Black people to stand for the National Anthem and revere it with respect (a song that has irrefutable nodes to racism and slavery in the third verse) understand what you are asking. When asking Black people to trust the country the same way that White people do, think about with the advent of technology, the sharing of information, the awakening and true understanding of what this country has done and continues to do to Black people, also understand the recent phenomenon in regards to pushing back. Understand that the very men who pushed for America to be the land of freedom, the very people who created the educational system, health system, the criminal justice system, the way in which our economy works, the way in which our country works as a whole, never intended for Black people to enjoy the same freedoms as everyone else. Due to this fact, that there has never been, and will never be, a *perfect union* in the United

States of America.

The perfect union that Barack Obama spoke about in 2008 sounded amazing. He was, and still is one of my personal heroes. This man, who later went on to become president of the United States of America, eloquently spoke about how he cannot condemn those who he loves for saying things that he does not agree with because that is the fabric of our nation. Black people, White people, brown people, and everyone else in between pull our nation forward together. Jules Vel, of *Medium,* said it best. "Obama's speech highlighted the issue of racial tension in America while also seeking to give context to Wright's statements. To begin, he quoted the section of the Preamble after which the speech was named, "We the people, in order to form *a more perfect union.*" Pointing out the proximity to Independence Hall, where the Constitution was signed, he asserted that slavery and legalized discrimination in our past conflict with the constitutional ideals of liberty, justice, and equal citizenship under the law. To atone for these "sins," he argued, we could perfect America by setting aside personal differences and uniting against shared social issues. Among these social issues is deep-seated anger in Black communities, which Obama attributed to the lasting effects of historic discrimination. He also recognized resentment by White immigrants who did not perpetuate Black-White racial tensions but receive blame based on their skin color. Though he acknowledged their legitimacy, he cautioned that harboring such feelings would prevent us from achieving unity.

Appealing to the American motto, *"E Pluribus Unum,"* or "out of many, [we are] one," Obama insisted unification is woven into American conscience. Labeling himself an unconventional candidate because of his multiethnic background, he expressed admiration for "commanding victories" in predominantly White states, and in South Carolina, where he garnered support from Black and White Americans alike. This, he inferred, shows America's hunger for unity. Ultimately, he maintained that by moving beyond America's "racial stalemate" and addressing shared social problems (consequences of the past), we could achieve "a more perfect union."

While the speech was great, the actions that followed President Obama, the first Black president in the history of our nation, showed that we still have a long way to go. From the protestors who adamantly and blatantly displayed their racism towards him. To the people who said that by him speaking on an issue like the murdering of Trayvon Martin, was setting our nation back in regard to race relations, *we the people*, were a long way from being one. I would imagine if you asked President Obama today, even with the outright hatred that he received in office, if he loved his country, he would respond just as I would. I love our country, flaws and all.

In 2020, the COVID19 (Coronavirus) pandemic has exposed the country as a whole to something that if we are being honest with each other, we have known all along. When America gets a cold, Black people get Pneumonia.

In some instances, such as Washington D.C., Black people make up less than half of the city's population but represent nearly 80% of the COVID19 cases. About 70% of the people who died in the District had hypertension. About half had diabetes, and studies show that people are far more likely to have these health issues if they are Black. While it is easy to blame Black people for their health situations, doing so absolves the structures that have created these situations. Structures, like discrimination, has stymied development. These structures limit access to healthy foods, create food deserts, and create barriers to amenities and employment. As a whole, prior to the pandemic, if a person lives in Ward 8 (which is 90% Black) you were expected to live nearly 15 years less than someone who lives in Ward 3, where 80% of residents are White.

Decades of structural racism in economic, educational, and housing policies have produced a stark racial wealth gap in the United States. Prior to this pandemic, the typical Black households had a net worth of just $17,100, compared with the $171,000 held by the typical White household. Black households also have far less liquidity than their White counterparts. Without wealth and liquidity, households may be unable to cover unexpected expenses and withstand long-term negative income shocks. Many of the federal homeownership and housing affordability policies of the 20th century disproportionately benefited White households while excluding households of color. Today, 73 percent of White families own their own home, compared with just 41 percent of Black families, according to a CAP analysis of U.S. Census Bureau data. Even when people of color are able to purchase their own homes, they often have to pay higher mortgage rates than their White neighbors. Renters of color are also at much higher risk of eviction. The COVID-19 pandemic will likely only exacerbate these disparities, as people of color are less likely to maintain steady incomes and to be able to depend on existing wealth to get through the current economic emergency.

The Ahmaud Arbery case, a situation in which a young Black man was brutally murdered by White vigilantes while jogging, exposed on a wide scale what most of us have known all along. There are many places in America where it is not safe to be Black. There was a post that was trending on social media that spoke volumes. It read:

"We can't go jogging (#AhmaudArbery).
We can't relax in the comfort of our own homes
(#BothemJean and #AtatianaJefferson).
We can't ask for help after being in a car crash
(#JonathanFerrell and #RenishaMcBride). We
can't have a cellphone (#StephonClark).
We can't leave a party to get to safety (#JordanEdwards).

We can't play loud music (#JordanDavis).
We can't sell CD's (#AltonSterling).
We can't sleep (#AiyanaJones)
We can't walk from the corner store (#MikeBrown).
We can't play cops and robbers (#TamirRice).
We can't go to church (#Charleston9).
We can't walk home with Skittles (#TrayvonMartin).
We can't hold a hair brush while leaving our own bachelor party (#SeanBell).
We can't party on New Years (#OscarGrant).
We can't get a normal traffic ticket (#SandraBland). We can't lawfully carry a weapon (#PhilandoCastile). We can't break down on a public road with car problems (#CoreyJones).
We can't shop at Walmart (#JohnCrawford) .
We can't have a disabled vehicle (#TerrenceCrutcher).
We can't read a book in our own car (#KeithScott).
We can't be a 10yr old walking with our grandfather (#CliffordGlover).
We can't decorate for a party (#ClaudeReese).
We can't ask a cop a question (#RandyEvans).
We can't cash our check in peace (#YvonneSmallwood).
We can't take out our wallet (#AmadouDiallo).
We can't run (#WalterScott).
We can't breathe (#EricGarner).
We can't live (#FreddieGray)."

I say this as a Black man, the great-great-grandson of enslaved Africans, and a person who still loves our country; our country has never been, and never will be united. That being said, just because something isn't perfect, or just because our past and in some instances our present is bad, doesn't mean that we don't have a responsibility to fight for what is right, for what is just, and for what is better for all.

In the land of the home of the free, as the individuals who are from where I live today described, ironically, the systems that they created are being carried out in many ways just as they were when they were alive.

To that point, what happens when people are sick and tired of being sick and tired? What happens when people read self-help books, learn more about the plights of others, feel invigorated to do something?

More often than not, they mull it over, think about it, maybe mention it here or there, but it is simply information retained. It's a level of knowledge that is now in their mind, has been retained, and will subsequently be a topic that they research and look into. More books about the topic of race relations, White Supremacy, systemic oppression, and the like will likely be consumed. Most people then attend a few talks about the need for the improvement of race relations, but unfortunately, that is the extent of where it goes.

What happens when we decide to do a little more?

What does doing a little more look like?

Every single person has to get to a point in which they are willing to decide to answer the internal question of "What am I going to do?" More specifically, what am I going to do in order to improve race relations in my neighborhood, in my community, in my city, in my state, in my country? In my opinion, all of these questions have to be asked in the most simplistic form first. As an individual are you willing to have the difficult conversations with yourself about your own bias? This is for both Black and White people. This is for any person of any race, religion, socioeconomic background, or any other identifier or label that people place on us to separate or divide us. When no one else is looking, when you wake up to brush your teeth in the morning, when you are in your few moments of solitude, are you willing to address the matters of race, White Supremacy, or change the systems that be? Are you willing to step out of your comfort zone to address inequities? When you are at your family gatherings, are you willing to make things somewhat tense by speaking on topics that make people uncomfortable because they "just want to be happy" in their bubble and not think about the other stuff?

When we are sitting at the dinner table with our immediate family members how willing are we to speak to our spouse, our children, our parents about why we all have to stand up for racial justice? Are we willing to be the person in the family that is known as the one who is "always talking about race stuff", or is it easier to just sit idle and allow things to be as they have been? The courage to do the internal work and then use the tools and information that we have to confront family and close friends is one that many people shy away from.

You see, for a lot of us, we know right from wrong when it pertains to race, but actually speaking up about it in a way that leads to action is a different issue there in itself. So, what is the next step, for both Black and White people? Is it going out and protesting the next time you see a tragedy? Is it joining an organization? Is it spending your money? Is it running for office? Is it helping with a campaign? Is it educating your family? Is it speaking with your friends? Well, it can be a whole gambit of things. That's the purpose of this book. We all can do a few things, but we all have to DO SOMETHING! Some of us are introverts, and some of us are extroverts. Some of us are researchers, some of us are analysts, and some of us are speakers. In the fight against White Supremacy, we all have a role to play. We all have to do the internal work to figure out what it is that we will do specifically. Along the road to understanding our own bias, understanding how to make change, understanding how to fight back, we all will fight differently. That is ok. White Supremacy is a byproduct of a system. A system that was created to utilize race as a social construct to put different people against each other. We have to be wise enough to understand this construct, understand how the system works, and be ok with the fact that the system that was created is working exactly how it was designed to. Racism wasn't created yesterday, last year, or even 100 years ago. It will not be dissolved overnight, but we do have the ability to defeat it over time. Remember, patient with people, and impatient with progress.

Now go out and FIGHT BACK!

You can't just vote, you have to FIGHT BACK!

You can't just pray, you have to FIGHT BACK!

You can't just wish away White Supremacy, you have to FIGHT BACK!

Fight for George Floyd, for Breonna Taylor, for Emmet Till, for Sandra Bland, for every Black enslaved woman who was raped, had her children stolen, and was treated less than. Fight for every person who built this country but never received a dime in payment. Fight for every abolitionist who was killed for fighting back. Fight for every person who wanted to fight but couldn't. My children, your children, your nieces, my future great grandchildren, and your future great-great grandchildren are depending on you. For them, we owe them a *more perfect union*!

When White Supremacy Knocks, Fight Back!

ABOUT THE AUTHOR

Dr. Wes Bellamy, is a former Vice-Mayor and City Councilman in Charlottesville, Virginia, the Political Science Department Chairman at Virginia State University, the national Co-Chairman of *Our Black Party* – a political platform focused on advancing the needs of Black people in America, and one of the Global thought leaders of the Millennial Generation. Dr. Bellamy is the Managing Partner of New Emergence Consulting, an Equity and Policy consulting firm, and the National Public Policy Chairman of the 100 Black Men of America. He is the youngest individual ever elected to the Charlottesville City Council post, and he came into the national spotlight after helping to lead the effort to remove statues of Robert E. Lee and Stonewall Jackson from City Parks.

He developed a comprehensive plan, the "Equity Package," which included nearly $4 million in aid for marginalized communities, and pushed it through city council. He is the founder of the Black Millennial Political Convention, a Convention focused on bringing together African American millennials from across the country to collectively use their power to create change. He has been featured in the New York Times. Washington Post, USA Today, Huffington Post, and has made appearances, on CNN, MSNBC, PBS News Hour, NPR, The Breakfast Club, and On One with Angela Rye.

When White Supremacy Knocks, Fight Back!

When White Supremacy Knocks, Fight Back!

Made in the USA
Middletown, DE
31 January 2022

59244392R00116